TICKET TO RIDE

The Extraordinary Diary
of THE BEATLES' Last Tour

TICKET TO RIDE

The Extraordinary Diary
of THE BEATLES' Last Tour

BARRY TASHIAN

DOWLING
PRESS, INC.

Publication date: January, 1997

Additional copies available by calling 1-800-409-7277

All other inquiries: 1-615-783-1668

Cover design: Mary Mazer, Art That Works, San Diego, California

Design, typography, and text production:
  Christine Shook, TypeByte Graphix

ISBN: 0-9646452-4-6

Dowling Press, Inc.
3200 West End Avenue, Suite 500
Nashville, Tennessee 37203
(615) 783-1668

For Daniel and Carl

ACKNOWLEDGEMENTS

■ I would like to express my gratitude to the dozens of people who contributed photographs, memorabilia and personal recollections to this book. Many people around the U.S. and abroad were very helpful to me in various ways: My father, Mel Tashian, of Articulate Graphics, New York, who suggested I keep a journal on the 1966 Beatles' tour, and who assisted with the creative design; Ed Freeman; Chip Bachrach; Don Cusic; Jean Elshtain; Barbara Bennett; Sid Bernstein; Nat Weiss; Peter Doggett, *Record Collector Magazine*, U.K.; Jeanne Kimball; Fred Straub; Eric Lefcowitz; Susan Madden, KBCS, Seattle; Vern Miller, Bill Briggs, N.D. Smart (The Remains); Tom Dawes, Don Dannemann, Earle Pickens, Marty Fried (The Cyrkle); Peter Guralnick; Erik Lindgren;

Andrew Rogers; Bill Finneran; Michael Holt; Hugh Holt; Mike Sachetti; Reggie Mays; Steve Frye; Pat MacMurray; Gordon and Becky Blackley; Gary Brown, Australia; Jim Meehan; Andrew Teton; Gary Parker; Mike Friedman; Jamie Adams; Rachel Brenner; Sue Dolan; Chet Snedden, American Airlines; Peter Ishkanian; Sohmer Hooker; Mark Staycer, WTCM, Traverse City; Frank Caiazzo; David H. Arnold, Jr.; Michael Shulman, Archive Photos, New-York; Andy Babiuk; Michael Ochs, Archives; Rodney Bingenheimer; John Koenig, *Discovery Magazine*; Mike Smythe; Allenette Douglas, Phonoluxe Records, Nashville; Tommy Goldsmith, *The Nashville Banner*; Bill and Terry Hanley, Hanley Sound, Boston; Bobby Hebb; Hugh Jones, Cellophane Square Records, Seattle; Tony Newman, Sounds Incorporated; Susannah Speisal, Florentine Films; Mike Voltz, Gibson Guitars; John Weisberger; Terry Moses; Naomi Soule, KDHX, St.Louis; Mark Richman; Bill King; Charles F. Rosenay; Peter Fuller, *Chicago Sun-Times*; Ray Fausher; Mitch McGreary; Dan Brooks; Peter Miniachi, Beatlemania, Toronto; Tony Spataro; Bruce Turner; Neal Skok; Daniel Cooper; Peter Anastasi.

Special thanks go to the following libraries:
  The Memphis Public Library
  The Cincinnati Public Library
  The Boston Public Library

To my publisher, Maryglenn McCombs of Dowling Press, for her support, organization and direction.

For help with creativity, design, technical advice and production, I am grateful to Christine Shook of TypeByte Graphix.

For research, thanks to Phil Nel.

I would especially like to thank Cecelia Tichi, an extraordinary English professor and friend, who suggested I do this book in the first place. She was very encouraging throughout the eighteen months of putting it together.

No one took a greater interest however, nor helped more in the day-to-day progress of this book than my wife, Holly Paige Tashian. I owe my affection and deepest gratitude to her, for her energy and enthusiasm throughout this endeavor.

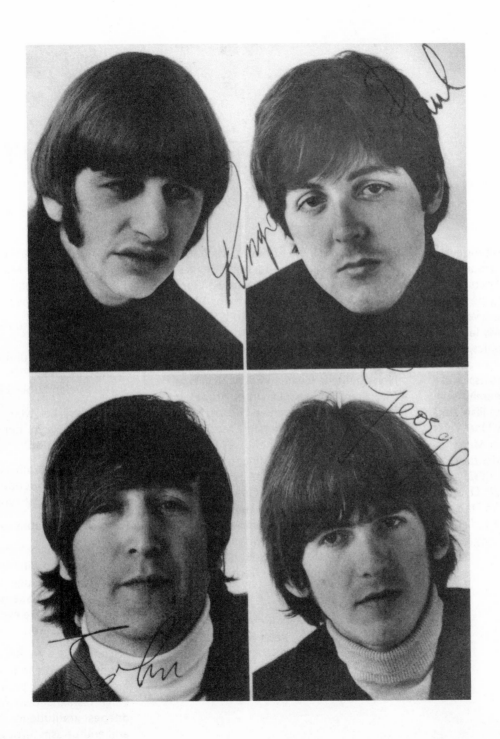

PREFACE

■ Opening for The Beatles was not an easy task. But that was my job for nineteen shows with The Beatles as leader of The Remains. Over the years, many people have suggested I write a book about my experiences on the 1966 Beatles' tour, but it was only recently that I took the idea seriously. My experience *was* unique. I had traveled with The Beatles during their very last tour. I was in their hotel rooms with them, looking out of the windows at the crowds in the streets below. We listened to records together. I ate, drank, smoked, and talked with The Beatles daily, and shared some very close personal moments with them. This was an experience that only a handful of people ever had.

For me, the tour was a life changing adventure I'll never forget. The Beatles shared their stage with me.

As it turned out, no one ever saw them in concert again. Fortunately, my dad suggested that I keep a journal of the tour, which I did, somewhat begrudgingly. I wrote in that journal every day of the tour, on the the planes, limousines, buses, and in hotel rooms. Now, of course, I see the wisdom in his suggestion. For, without it, this book would not exist.

In this book, along with my journal, I've included many unpublished photographs from numerous sources; memorabilia from my collection, as well as from generous people around the country; fan recollections from those who went to The Beatles' concerts; and newspaper articles from around the country. I have also included the excellect writing of Judith Simms, editor of *TeenSet* magazine, who traveled with the press corps accompanying The Beatles, and wrote insightful city-by-city accounts of the entire tour.

My purpose in writing this book is to share with you the excitment, the electricity, the sights, and the sounds of that phenomenal August in 1966.

Ticket To Ride depicts the dramatic experiences of life on tour with The Beatles at the height of their popularity. It reveals facts and feelings from my perspective as a tour musician who traveled close to The Beatles and associated with them on personal and professional levels. It narrates, from an inside view, the events that took place; it vividly recreates the exhiliration of The Beatles' last tour.

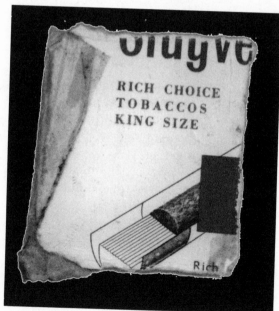

John Lennon's handwritten set list, written on the inside of
a Peter Stuyvesant cigarette pack. It includes all
eleven songs The Beatles played
on the 1966 tour.

INTRODUCTION

■ People often ask me how I got to go on tour with The Beatles. My answer is always, "Good timing and simple luck."

From an early age, I knew music was my passion. My grandmother was a passionate singer who was always singing around the house, and both of my parents were very musical. My mother played the piano and my father played drums in a dance band.

Between my family and the cultural influences which surrounded me, I had many role models. Watching Gene Autrey and Roy Rodgers, television's singing cowboys, inspired me greatly, and I picked up my first guitar when I was ten. In 1957, when I was in the seventh grade, artists like Elvis Presley, Bill Haley and Little

Richard were sweeping the nation and I started my own rock 'n roll band. We played at school dances, talent shows, and local concerts in Westport, Connecticut.

But, it was in 1959 that I got my first real break. I played with a group called The Ramblers and we had our first hit, a rock 'n roll instrumental called "Ramblin'." In the ninth grade, I got the opportunity to play on Dick Clark's *American Bandstand*. It was an amazing experience.

It wasn't until the summer after my freshman year at Boston University while I was in London, that I was introduced to the music of the Kinks and the Rolling Stones. When I returned to Boston in the Fall of 1964, along with three other students, we got together the band, The Remains. Within three months, we were recording for Columbia Records.

The Remains took a year off from Boston University to pursue music full-time; we had several top five hit records in the Boston area and felt we were ready. In 1966 we moved to New York City; it was, after all, the place to be. We performed on some very highly rated network TV shows including the *Ed Sullivan Show* and *Hulaballoo*. This was simply phenomenal considering that we had only regional success with our hits, "Why Do I Cry" and "Diddy Wah Diddy."

Less than four months after our relocation to New York our manager, John Kurland, asked us the most amazing question, "Would you guys like to go on tour with The Beatles?" Our answer was, of course, a collective "Groovy!"

The Remains were the perfect choice for The Beatles' tour since we had no national hit record and could assume the role of "backup band." This was a small price to pay for the national recognition we would gain

Sunday, December 26th, 1965

6:30 **(2)** • **"Pinocchio,"** musical adaptation of children's classic, presented by the Prince Street Players Ltd. (C)

(11) Ripcord (C)

(31) Magic Carpet

(47) Italian News

7:00 **(7)** • **Voyage To the Bottom of the Sea:** "Terror on Dinosaur Island," Richard Basehart, David Hedison (C)

(9) Death Valley Days (C)

(11) • **"Dr. Zhivago,"** ceremonies at world premiere of M.G.M. motion picture in New York City

(31) The Big Picture

(47) Favorite Novelas: This week "Almas En Ruina" (Spanish)

7:30 **(2)** • **My Favorite Martian:** Ray Walston, Bill Bixby

(4) • **Walt Disney;** "A Present for Donald," musical tour of Latin America (C)

(9) Big Preview: "David and Goliath" (1961), Orson Welles. Dismal dubbed epic (C)

(31) World of the Arts

8:00 **(2)** • **Ed Sullivan Show:** Sergio Franchi, Leontyne Price, The Remains, Jack Carter, and Peter Gennaro (C)

by "opening" for The Beatles. We would open each concert by playing twenty minutes of our own music before backing up two other acts, Bobby Hebb and The Ronettes. The tour was to cover fourteen North American cities during August, 1966, in what would become eighteen of the most memorable days of my life.

As we celebrated winning our place on the upcoming Beatles' North American tour, The Remains suddenly faced a major dilemma. Our drummer, who was reluctant to leave Boston in the first place, decided not to go with us on The Beatles' tour, and consequently quit the band. At the last minute, we found a seventeen-year-old replacement drummer, N.D. Smart. Opening for The Beatles in Chicago was the first time we performed with the new drummer—13,000 people saw our debut.

The Beatles themselves faced greater problems, and almost cancelled the tour before it even began. It appeared that they had entered a dangerous position, for, while Beatlemania was at its peak, they had ignited the flames of controversy, and were seen by many in the U.S. as problematic. In 1964 and

1965, during their initial popularity in the U.S., The Beatles had personified good fun. *The Saturday Evening Post* wrote that The Beatles had "a bouncy irreverence" that gave us "a release from austere inhibitions." One American girl was quoted saying, "I'd hate to have grown up when there weren't any Beatles."

However, the political unrest of the time, due to the social revolution, gained momentum during the mid-sixties. The drug culture had begun; the baby boomers were in college and "turning on." This young generation, which was growing in number, had begun to reject the values of the establishment. Social rules were changing and young people cried out for political and sexual freedom. British writer and cultural analyst James Morris wrote, "The Beatles have been the minstrels of this emancipation." The Beatles had been instrumental in starting the social revolution of the sixties, and Beatlemania had reached a point where, at many of their concerts, the words of their songs could not be heard above the screaming fans. Worldwide, their public loved them so much that The Beatles became prisoners of their own

The original Remains—(left to right) Bill Briggs, keyboard, vocals; Vern Miller, bass, vocals; Barry Tashian, guitar, vocals; and Chip Damiani, drums.

fame. For The Beatles, touring was becoming troublesome, as well as dangerous.

But, dangerous mobs of fans were not their only problem. In June and July of 1966, The Beatles had survived some difficult experiences touring the Far East. Due to misunderstandings involving Asian royalty, governments and traditions, The Beatles found themselves in situations that were virtually life threatening.

In addition, the misquoted statement by John Lennon that The Beatles were "more popular than Jesus," was taken so seriously in America that Beatle record-burning parties were organized. However, despite the controversy, The Beatles arrived in Chicago on August 12, 1966, and the tour began.

Recalling the 1966 Beatles' tour, one memory stands out. I can still feel the excitement. There I was, twenty-one years old, standing in the darkened dugout of Shea Stadium at showtime, ready to walk out to center stage on second base for my fif-

teenth show opening for The Beatles. I could feel the overwhelming anticipation of 50,000 fans. The feeling in that stadium, with the brilliant spotlights illuminating the entire field, was more intense than any words or pictures can ever express. Nonetheless, I hope that this book will bring alive, once again, the electrifying excitement of The Beatles' last tour.

The Remains as they appeared on tour with The Beatles. (Left to right) Bill Briggs, Vern Miller, N.D. Smart, and Barry Tashian.

The supporting acts for The Beatles' tour

THE CYRKLE
four undergraduates from Lafayette University. Top: Earle Pickens, piano, vocals; Marty Fried, drums; Bottom: Don Dannemann, guitar, vocals; and Tom Dawes, bass, guitar, and vocals. The Cyrkle, who were co-managed by Brian Epstein and Nat Weiss, had a hit record with "Red Rubber Ball," and had just released "Turn Down Day."

BOBBY HEBB
from Nashville, Tennesssee. Wrote and recorded his big hit, "Sunny," which was in the top of the charts in August, '66.

THE RONETTES
(Ronnie Spector was not on the tour, her cousin Elaine stood in for her); Estelle Bennett, Nedra Talley, and Elaine. The Ronettes were the prime example of Phil Spector's "Wall of Sound." Two of their big hits were: "Da Doo Ron Ron," and "Be My Baby."

The Beatles' Original Tour Schedule

Date	City	Venue	# of Shows
August 12	Chicago	International Amphitheatre	2 (4 & 8 P.M.)
August 13	Detroit	Olympia Stadium	2 (4 & 8 P.M.)
August 14	Cleveland	Municipal Stadium	1 (8 P.M.)
August 15	Washington	Stadium	1 (8 P.M.)
August 16	Philadelphia	Stadium	1 (8 P.M.)
August 17	Toronto	Maple Leaf Gardens	2 (4 & 8 P.M.)
August 18	Boston	Suffolk Downs Racetrack	1 (8 P.M.)
August 19	Memphis	Coliseum	2 (4 & 8 P.M.)
August 20	Cincinnati	Crosley Field	1 (8 P.M.)
August 21	St. Louis	Busch Stadium	1 (8 P.M.)
August 23	New York	Shea Stadium	1 (8 P.M.)
August 25	Seattle	Coliseum	2 (4 & 8 P.M.)
August 28	Los Angeles	Dodger Stadium	1 (8 P.M.)
August 29	San Francisco	Candlestick Park	1 (8 P.M.)

The Beatles' 1966 North American Tour

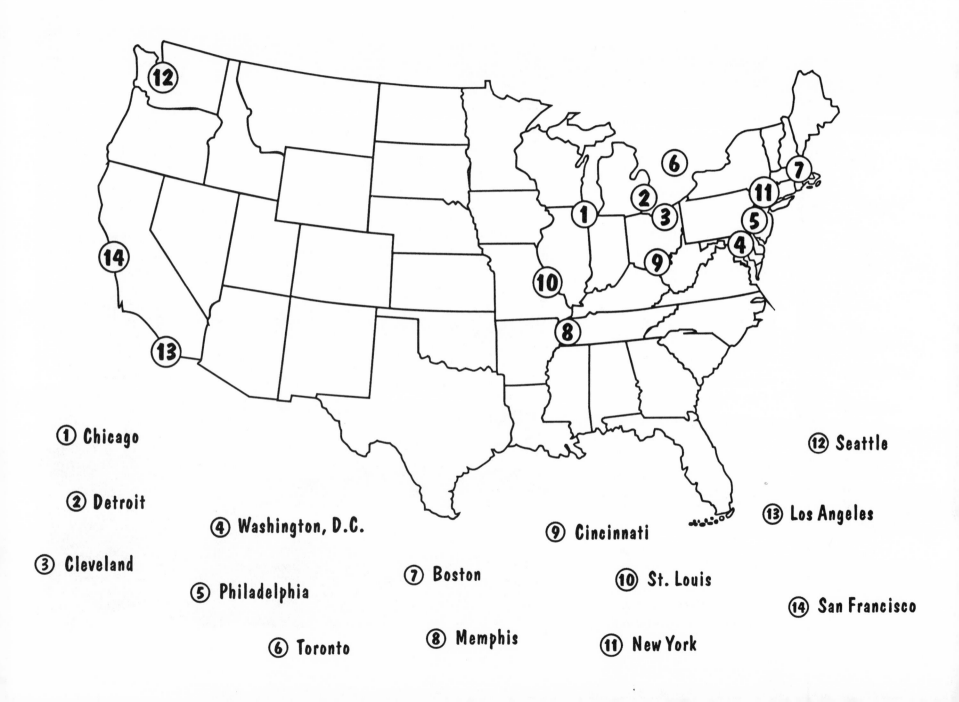

① Chicago

② Detroit

③ Cleveland

④ Washington, D.C.

⑤ Philadelphia

⑥ Toronto

⑦ Boston

⑧ Memphis

⑨ Cincinnati

⑩ St. Louis

⑪ New York

⑫ Seattle

⑬ Los Angeles

⑭ San Francisco

CHICAGO

■ TODAY

288,000 military men are now stationed in Vietnam. President Lyndon Johnson announced that victory could be possible in two years through a substantial increase in the number of troops employed in the war.

In Saigon, the U.S. Air Force mistakenly attacked an American Coast Guard cutter in the second case of erroneous identification this week. One captain was killed and five others were wounded.

In Chicago, 725 civil rights demonstrators marched though the all-white Ashburn section of Chicago for an open-housing demonstration. One thousand helmeted police lined the streets. The only disturbance came from bands of white teenagers setting off cherry bombs. The Reverend Jesse Jackson, aid to Dr. Martin Luther King, Jr., praised the police and community leaders for the mostly peaceful march.

This year Pampers Disposable Diapers were introduced.

Downtown Chicago

Journal

Thursday, August 11, 1966:

Arrived here yesterday from New York, via Toronto, on Air Canada, due to the U.S. Airline Strike. Weather: rainy, windy, dirty, August day. People here look very straight, very hardworking. Some look outraged at the sight of us long-haired, hot rod, hippie-type rock 'n rollers. For The Beatles' tour, the Fender Company has given us free guitars and amplifiers, which we picked up on the way to the International Amphitheatre.

    Are we *good* enough to back The Ronettes and Bobby Hebb? Their material is tough, challenging; Hebb's "Sunny" has a lot of chord changes. And, The Ronettes' records are the prime example of Phil Spector's "Wall of Sound" with layers of multi-tracked instruments— we're just a *four-piece* band! Plus, rumor has it that Phil Spector was dismissive and insulting when he heard The Remains would back The Ronettes. No vote of confidence there.

    The Remains vowed never to back up other acts! But, for The Beatles' tour... well... we can make an exception. The rehearsal with The Ronettes and Bobby Hebb went okay. So far, so good. It's too bad Ronnie isn't on this tour. She *is* the Ronettes voice! Her cousin, Elaine, is standing in for her.

Thursday, August 11th, *The Astor Towers, Chicago*

The Beatles arrived from London on a commercial Pan Am flight. They were escorted directly to the Astor Towers Hotel for their first press conference. The main subject being John Lennon's comments about being more popular than Jesus.

"I'm sorry I said what I said because of the mess it made," John said. "I suppose if I said television was more popular than Jesus, I would have got away with it. I am sorry I opened my mouth... I'm not anti-God, anti-Christ, or anti-religion. I was not knocking it [religion]. I was not saying we were greater or better."

Reporters called it the public apology of the year.

"I do believe Christianity is shrinking, that people are losing contact with it. But, we deplore this," Lennon said. He continued, "I was worried stiff when I found out it had become so serious. I'm sorry for the mess it's made. There'll be no more words. I panicked when I first heard about the uproar. I said, 'I'm not going to America at all.' We could have hidden away, but we decided to come and try to straighten it out. That interview was with a friend of mine. It was a long one, in depth. And, I wasn't thinking in terms of public relations."

Hundreds of teenage girls and members of the press milled around the Ascot Towers Hotel at 1300 North Ascot, waiting for a glimpse of The Beatles, but The Beatles were secretly moved to the Ascot Motel on South Michigan for the night.

Astor Towers Hotel—Chicago

The Beatles after their first press conference during the tour.

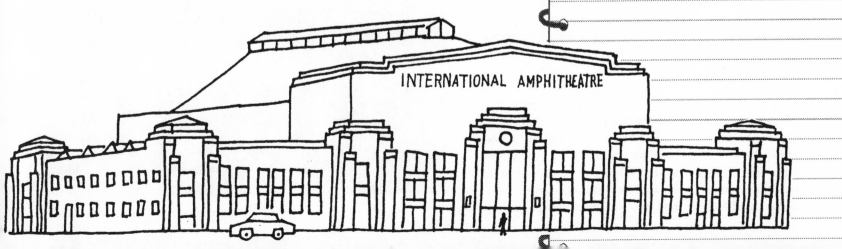

The Remains rehearse at the International Amphitheatre
in Chicago for opening night of The Beatles' tour.

Journal

The Beatles are giving a press conference at the Astor Towers Hotel. Meanwhile, we rehearse on-stage in the International Amphitheatre, which smells of cattle because the Chicago Stockyard is right next door. The stage is about six feet high and draped with gold curtains. I'm left alone for a few minutes in the huge hall with thousands of vacant seats. It's a weird feeling, anticipation in this big void! Tomorrow is the first show.

Friday, August 12, 1966:
On the way to the show our limousine was mobbed by fans, even though The Beatles weren't even with us— felt like I was in a scene from *A Hard Day's Night!* Being in a car that's swarmed by girls screaming, pounding on the windows, climbing on the fenders, and rocking the car is a new experience for me! I know the fans wanted The Beatles, but it's fun to imagine they were after us.

INTERNATIONAL AMPHITHEATRE

ON TOUR

with

THE Beatles

*by Judith Sims,
Editor, TeenSet Magazine*

■ Departing Los Angeles for Chicago, I arrived on the scene and noticed that several hundred teenagers had beat me to it. The Astor Towers was surrounded by milling, screaming girls (and boys), and milling, yelling policemen. I couldn't help wondering where all those adults who had predicted the demise of Beatlemania were. No doubt they couldn't get through the crowds.

Getting into the hotel was quite a feat. I finally convinced the officer in charge of the revolving door that I really did have business there; I had to get in to meet Beatles' press officer Tony Barrow so that I could get the proper identification which would have admitted me in the first place!

On the way to the 28th floor rendezvous with Tony, the elevator stopped at the 24th floor, and four Beatles walked in. All wit and pluck deserted me (not an unusual circumstance in itself), and I just stared for three floors. I was a bit incoherent when Tony handed me the open-all-doors-we-hope red tour pass. He told me just to "float" until press conference time, but I was way ahead of him.

The Beatles' Chicago press conference was the first of their tour, and the center of attention for the whole nation—practically the whole world. Just a few weeks before the tour, John Lennon's widely publicized comments on the respective Jesus/Beatles popularity had stirred up controversy beyond sensibility, and there were rumors that performances would be picketed, boycotted, or canceled. Chicago would be the first time, the press would or could confront John.

The "controversy question" was the first one asked, and John answered directly, sensibly, and humbly. He explained that his comment had been misinterpreted. A close friend had been interviewing him and they had merely been discussing meaningful problems. He had been deploring the fact that The Beatles seem to be more popular than Jesus. He also stated that he used The Beatles in his comparison because The Beatles are what he knows best; he could just as easily have said television, or movies, or radio. He said he was indeed sorry that it had made so many people unhappy, because that was certainly not his intention.

Although John was asked this question at every press conference, the attitude of the press in attendance was fairly consistent—sympathetic and understanding. In several cases there were groans of disgust when the question was asked. Many people considered it a dead issue two minutes after John answered it the first time. They were right.

The Chicago press conference quickly changed from tense anticipation to happy congeniality, and the working press got down to the business at hand—enjoying The Beatles. John confirmed that he would be making a movie without the others and firmly denied that this indicated he was leaving the group.

The one question which was most frequently asked in past years was noticeably ignored in Chicago—the Paul/Jane query.

Thursday night, after the con-

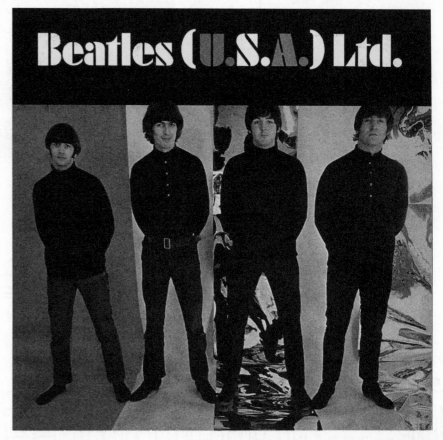

A program from The Beatles' 1966 tour

ference, The Beatles didn't leave their rooms, but Tony Barrow threw a get-together for the press party (disc jockeys and journalists) traveling with the group, and the tour was off to a good start.

The next day, Friday, was the first concert date at the Chicago Amphitheatre, which is unfortunately located next to the aromatic stockyards. No one really noticed because there was a much stronger, not to mention nicer, thing in the air—Beatlemania.

The lead off act was The Remains, who also served as backup group for Bobby Hebb and The Ronettes. This tour had some of the best supporting acts yet; The Cyrkle had just gone up the charts with "Red Rubber Ball," and "Turn Down Day" was on its way. Bobby Hebb's "Sunny" was number one during the tour. After The Ronettes' rousing closer of their "What'd I Say," there was always a brief intermission of about fifteen minutes while The Beatles' equipment manager, Malcolm Evans, assisted usually by Alfie Bicknell (another road manager) and the road managers of The Remains and The Cyrkle, set the stage for the "really big shew." When all was ready, Mal would signal the disc jockeys, who would then say, "And now . . . The Beatles!" From that point, all of us reverted to sign language to communicate, because no amount of shouting could be heard over any Beatle audience.

In Chicago we were sitting behind and to the right of the stage,

and the roar was deafening. For at least fifteen minutes after the show, our ears were ringing and our eyes were still seeing exploding flashbulbs. It's a wonder The Beatles can see or hear at all after going through that so often.

Between the two Chicago performances there was a "taping session" in the boys' room (Through-out the tour they were referred to collectively as "the boys"). This was my first person-to-person contact, except for the timid elevator episode; so, I'm sure that I'll be forgiven if I didn't get the most accurate notes in the world. There were no formal introductions—most of the press party had been on last year's tour, so they just picked up where they had left off, and everyone sort of wandered around from Beatle to Beatle, tape recorders whirring away. Ringo was sitting cross-legged on a couch in front of a coffee table piled high with gifts from fans (Gifts were *everywhere*.). George was stretched out on another couch; John was seated behind a desk; and Paul was on a chair near the desk. They were surrounded by tape recorders, and the whole thing was most informal. The rule followed for taping sessions was, grab the closest Beatle and talk into the microphone, except that several people usually converged on one Beatle at a time. It made for some very interesting tapes!

Both Chicago concerts were a bit of a success (rather!).

Journal

Big crimp in our plans, though. We arrived at the show to find the "Powers-That-Be" decided The Remains could not use any Fender equipment, but Vox amplifiers only. (The Beatles' endorsement with Vox probably arranged this.) Vox brought some solid-state amplifiers made in the U.S. by the Thomas Organ Company for us to use and our nice Fender equipment got shipped back to New York.

Meanwhile, our sound company from Boston (Hanley Sound) drove to Chicago to do the show with us. They pulled their truck right into the Amphitheatre, unloaded, and set up their state-of-the-art sound equipment right beside the in-house P.A. system. What a joke. The in-house stuff was so archaic next to our powerful amps, good mics, and AltecVoice of the theater speakers.

Right before the first show, Brian Epstein looked at the two sound systems and decided that The Beatles should go with OUR system. So, The Beatles hired Bill Hanley to do the sound for part of the tour!

Beatles: A Sound Analysis

by Glenna Syse

You have to see it to believe it, because it is not the kind of thing you believe by hearing.

These conclusions are not sociological, they are medical. When you plug over 10,000 young female larynxes into The Beatles' circuit, you produce a vibration that causes a disease called labyrinthitis, which is an inflammation of the inner ear that sometimes results in loss of balance. It is an ailment that seems to affect only those age 15, and that is why all the adults leaving the International Amphitheatre Friday seemed to be listing.

I am what is laughingly known as adult, and that is why I am writing this at an angle. If you have trouble reading it, rotate the page thirty-five degrees to the right.

In the interests of equilibrium, you should know this is a review of The Beatles who gave two concerts Friday at the International Amphitheatre. The gross was $136,000.

In my memory, it is the only event I have reported upon by using paper and pencil to ask questions. I wrote a note to a fireman, "How many firemen?" Over the din, he took my pencil and wrote "100 firemen." I got my hot dog by pointing to it.

What did they sing? Well, it was all over and the diminuendo left only the sounds of a few sobs. I got my answers from three fourteen-year-olds—Kathy, Sue and Pat. They said The Beatles sang "Rock 'N Roll Music," "She's a Woman," "If I Needed Someone," "Day Tripper," "Baby's in Black," "I Feel Fine," "Yesterday," "I Wanna Be Your Man," "Nowhere Man," "Paperback Writer" and "Long Tall Sally." How they know is one of the miracles of the five senses. Three shrewd young ladies they were. They expressed the belief that a concert such as this promotes record sales. Because, if you can't hear it, you go out and buy it and listen to it at home.

And, one of the girls had the final say on John Lennon's now notorious remarks.

"I'm a minister's daughter and I go to church three times a week and I love The Beatles. I think what they meant was they may be more popular than Jesus but they are not better than Jesus."

Strictly as a production, the concert was rather haphazard, except in matters of security. Two hundred Andy Frain ushers were inside along with 100 firemen and 84 Burns detectives. They formed a solid line in front of the stage and countered hysteria by flashing lights into the anguished, screaming faces.

The stage was far too small to accommodate the amplification apparently necessary for this 20th century sound.

There was a tense gap between the acts that preceded the headliners and The Beatles themselves. And, The Beatles' stage manager got very red in the face as he moved the amplifiers and machines around. Even when they were hooked up, they didn't always work. In moments of adjustment, John Lennon did a little dance that created a response that must have been heard by all the cattle for blocks around.

The reaction to The Beatles' appearance was tumultuous, a word that seems a total understatement. If this is what happens when The Beatles are banned, what do you suppose would happen if they were abolished?

The Beatles were preceded by The Remains, The Ronettes, The Cyrkle, and Bobby Hebb—who presented a cheerful two hours of insanity before the main bout. One final note. Do The Beatles have a new sound? It's a purely academic question.

THE BEATLES
August 12 - 3:00 & 7:00 P.M.
INTERNATIONAL AMPHITHEATRE
PLUS
THE CYRKLE   **THE RONETTES**
THE REMAINS   **BOBBY HEBB**
A FEW TICKETS AVAILABLE
AT McCORMICK PLACE BOX OFFICE

John and Paul at the International
Amphitheatre in Chicago.

Journal

WHAT AN AMAZING FEELING! We've just
played for a total of 25,000 people today!
It's hard to believe... but we did it and we're
still alive!! WOW!

On their way to the stage, The Beatles
walked past me single file, with Brian Epstein
following them. Ringo glanced across and said
hello. I made eye contact with a Beatle!

Brian Epstein introduced himself to me
and we shook hands.

Then, The Beatles went on stage and all
hell broke loose! The Beatles and the fans
were having a good time until George's
amplifier got unplugged by mistake.
Fortunately, it only took a minute to discover
the problem.

We got back to the Sherman House, room
456. Gotta get some sleep. We need to be in
the lobby at 8 A.M. to get to Detroit. What an
AMAZING DAY!

INTERNATIONAL AMPHITHEATRE
42nd and Halsted Streets — Chicago
THE ARCUS TICKET CO. CHICAGO
MEZZANINE
R 6 13
AUG.
12
1966
FRIDAY 7:30 p.m.
THE BEATLES
No Refunds-No Exchanges
ADMISSION $4.75

FANS REFLECT
REFLECT

■ The 1966 Beatles' tour of America turned out to be their final tour ever, and in many ways, you could see it coming. It had been two years since the fireworks of Beatlemania had initially exploded in America. While The Beatles' albums were becoming increasingly sophisticated (<u>Rubber Soul</u> and <u>Revolver</u>), their concert tours had become even more of a carnival. One factor was the overpowering screaming fans who, by and large, remained fairly oblivious to the actual musical performance. Another factor was the woefully inadequate P.A. and stage equipment, crudely adapted from sports stadium usage. In many cases, The Beatles were left in a position of barely being able to hear themselves. Naturally, after years of grinding out club dates in England and Germany, and the rocket ride of success that followed during the next two years, how exciting could it be for a band to give their 3,000th live performance of "She Loves You?" But, if any additional catalyst was needed to set off the chemical equation that would cause The Beatles to decide to hang it up in terms of touring, the straw that broke The Beatles' collective back was the firestorm of controversy that followed John Lennon's

widely quoted—and nearly universally misunderstood—statement: "The Beatles are bigger than Jesus."

The Beatles, who had been the darlings of the youth culture and media, were suddenly stunned to feel the wrath of misguided religious communities. John Lennon, who made the remark in a probing interview, was describing an erosion of values and sense of meaning. But, in the bewildering mass hysteria that followed months later, when the excerpted and inflammatory remarks became headlines in America, huge anti-Beatle rallies were held throughout the U.S., particularly in the South. The Beatles were roundly denounced and their records burned and trampled. In just a few years The Beatles went from breaking records to having their records broken.

On another level, this controversy threatened me personally. I had a priceless pair of tickets to see The Beatles' first concert of the new U.S. tour following the controversy. Suddenly, my world was rocked by a maternal encyclical from my Catholic girlfriend's mother: "No daughter of mine will see those godless punks." I really sweated that week, staying up to watch as a nervous Brian Epstein

(on *The Tonight Show*) endeavored to explain the indignity people felt with only limited success. When John Lennon himself was hauled before reporters at the start of the tour and painfully tried to explain what he had meant, he appeared concerned enough—if not contrite enough—to slacken at least some of the knee jerk response. At least my girlfriend was given permission to go!

By comparison, the concert was almost an anticlimax. I remember driving the Outer Drive in Chicago on the way to the International Amphitheatre to hear Bobby Hebb sing "Sunny." I knew he was on the bill with The Beatles, and it fueled my excitement. When my girlfriend, upon whom I had given this ultimate date, broke up with me a few weeks later, I developed a pathological hatred for "Sunny."

As for the concert, I believe that memory is somewhat plastic and changes over time. I have seen The Beatles' video from the Budokan in Tokyo from the same summer so many times, I think some of those images have migrated a bit into my own actual experience at the Chicago Amphitheatre. We were seated in the last row of the flat floor, so we didn't have a great angle or line of sight. The opening act dutifully, even enthusiastically, went through the thankless chore of "opening the show." In addition to Hebb was The Cyrkle ("Red Rubber Ball"), and I remember their distinction being that they were the only U.S. act managed by Brian Epstein (a mixed blessing, I imagine). The other band that made an impression was Barry & The Remains. I was kind of fascinated by them. I had never heard of this band, yet they were opening for The Beatles. The lead singer reminded me a bit of Gerry Marsden (of Gerry and the Pacemakers) whom I liked. And, he played a ridiculously weird Al Caiola model Epiphone guitar which seemed to have a Wurlitzer organ effects panel grafted on it. I remember their performance as being rootsy and a lot grittier than the squeaky sound of The Cyrkle. I did think that they were cool, but naturally my main focus was The Beatles.

What can I say about their performance? Although I couldn't often hear it, I dug it enormously, nonetheless. Just the few scraps and recognizable riffs from "Paperback Writer," "She's a Woman," "I Feel Fine" — the songs from the more recent repertoire — were overpoweringly exciting to hear. I had seen The Beatles the year before in Comiskey Park and that was exciting, but the songs in this set were so much more marvelous to me — the vision of them in the flesh, their cool new stage outfits, the shirts with the long pointy collars, the odd sight of both George and John playing identical sunburst Epiphone Casino guitars rather than the Rickenbacker and Gretsch I had come to know. Just as with my first Beatles concert, I couldn't believe it was them. I'm sure that's why so many millions screamed in their presence.

As we drove home later, with my head still swimming with it all, I promised myself I would try to remember every detail so I could always access it perfectly — a wonderful teenage fantasy about trapping memories, about capturing lightning in a bottle. Many of the details of that concert have eroded since then, but I still have an indelible sense in my very marrow of how exciting it was.

—Andrew Teton

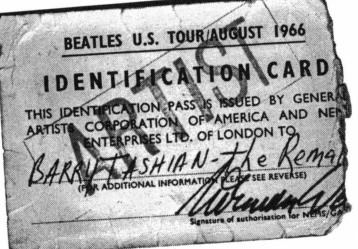

The Remains, with Don Dannemann of The Cyrkle, tune up backstage before the first concert.

I saw The Beatles twice in Chicago. I still have the ticket stubs. The only two things I really remember are, not hearing much unless you put your fingers in your ears, and in Comisky Park ('65) there were guys walking around in Beatle suits. We all thought it was *them* just walking around.

—MBR

■ TODAY . . .

The Lunar Orbiter is on target to become the first American space-craft to circle the moon. Its mission is to take 320 close-up snapshots along the moon's equator to determine a future landing site for astronauts. The craft weighs 850 pounds.

The U.S. Senate requests an estimated 150,000 reserve troops be called to serve in Vietnam.

The Vatican City newspaper *L'Osservatore Romano*, accepted John Lennon's apology for his remarks about Jesus. The paper said there was some truth in his observations on atheism.

This year the Motion Picture Academy Awards (Oscars) went to:

Best Actor
  Paul Scofield,
  A Man For All Seasons;

Best Actress
  Elizabeth Taylor,
  Who's Afraid of Virginia Woolf?;

Best Supporting Actor
  Walter Matthau,
  The Fortune Cookie;

Best Supporting Actress
  Sandy Dennis,
  Who's Afraid of Virginia Woolf?;

Best Picture, 1966,
  A Man For All Seasons

General Motors Buildings—Detroit

The American Airlines Electra chartered for the tour—The Beatles' home away from home during their 1966 tour.

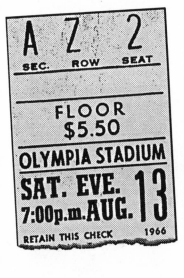

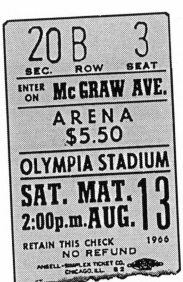

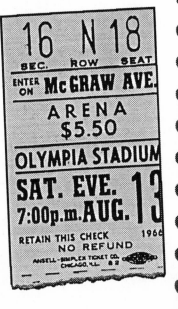

Journal

Saturday, August 13th
First Flight of the Tour:
Paul was the only Beatle up and around in flight, working his way slowly through the airplane, greeting people and chatting. The rest of The Beatles stayed in the back of the plane, in their own little area.

We had omelettes for breakfast on board. My coffee almost flew into the air in the various levels of air pockets. I gulped it down, though.

After landing, we taxied into a hangar away from the public terminal, and unloaded onto a chartered bus to take us to Detroit. We were escorted by three Wayne County Sheriff's cars to the city limits. At that point, six Detroit Police motorcycles took over and escorted us to Olympia Stadium. On the Ford Freeway, two carloads of girls tried to drive their cars in front of our bus, but the police forced them over to the shoulder of the road. Once in Detroit, we were greeted by a couple hundred people at Olympia Stadium. On the way into the press conference, John almost wiped out when he tripped over a photographer's tripod.

ON TOUR

with

THE BEATLES

by Judith Sims,
Editor, TeenSet Magazine

■ We flew to Detroit where there was a jumping crowd waiting at the airport. We transferred to a bus which took us to the stadium, and as we pulled into the parking lot The Beatles were asked to put their heads down so the mob wouldn't know they were in the bus. They didn't like that idea, Paul in particular refused to slouch down. The guards had quite a time keeping the fans back so we could get out of the bus. Once the fans caught a glimpse of a real live Beatle, it was pure bedlam.

Looking back, there really isn't a great deal I can say about each individual concert, because each one was fantastic. The Beatles themselves don't feel they are the greatest performers, but I know of no other act in pop music that I (or anyone, for that matter) could watch 18 times and love every minute of it. And without exception, the fans screamed, sobbed, yelled, waved signs, and just generally blew their minds. If Beatlemania is dying out, someone should tell all those fans about it!

From Detroit we climbed back on the bus for the ride to Cleveland. Since the bus had remained inside the stadium, there was no James Bondish sort of maneuver getting The Beatles out, as there would be in future adventures. The Beatles dashed from the stage to the bus—complete with stage suits and perspiring brows —and off we went. It was night and the lights were off at first; later I learned that the lights were off because four Beatles were changing clothes in the back of the bus!

It was an all-night ride straight through. At one point the bus pulled off the road in a Howard Johnson's parking lot for a rest stop. Several of us stood outside stretching while Wendy Hanson, Brian Epstein's assistant, went in the restaurant and bought "ice lollies," or ice cream bars, which we promptly consumed. The people inside were completely oblivious to the fact that the lonely betoweled figure sitting on the curb was George Harrison and that the group loitering beside the bus included Paul McCartney, Ringo Starr, Brian Epstein, and so on. A few couples walked by and never even glanced our way—but one woman and two young girls soon came charging up waving paper and pens. They informed Paul that they had been following the bus since Detroit, and asked for an autograph. He signed one, after which the woman demanded, "Now sign this one." To which Paul replied, "Is that an order?" She didn't get the hint, but she did get the autographs.

The Beatles enjoy playing to an unusually close audience at Olympia Stadium in Detroit.

Barry and Vern of The Remains onstage
at Olympia Stadium.

Journal

Olympia Stadium is a large indoor arena with the audience surrounding the stage. With the fans all around, we turned and smiled at the people behind us. (The girls smiled back.) The crowd seemed to like us as much as The Beatles! It was amazing!

We loved the feeling of intimacy here. It worked for us and helped us win the audience over. This was not an important factor for The Beatles because they don't need to prove themselves.

The Beatles' concert is really groovy, but also kind of scary. The crowd just goes completely nuts when The Beatles come into view. The sound of screaming humanity sounds like a rocket ship blasting off. I can't describe the sheer physical force of it. It's also an emotional thrill to be there to witness it! Even with all the security it seems like the crowd could at any moment crush them if they wanted to. It's scary.

Drove in the bus to Cleveland. En route we stopped at a Howard Johnson's, where some people walking by were surprised to see The Beatles out for a stretch near the bus.

Arrived in Cleveland at 3 A.M.— tired as hell! I'm going to sleep.

30,800 Jam Beatlefest at Olympia

by Jackie Korona

Detroit teenagers stuffed an estimated $100,000 into the pockets of The Beatles Saturday for the privilege of screaming so loudly they couldn't hear their idols sing.

By Beatle standards, the visit of the mop-topped quartet was routine:

• About 30,800 screeching enthusiasts shoved their way into Olympia Stadium for two shows —14,000 at the matinee and 16,800 at the evening performance—paying $5.50, $4.50 and $3.50 for a seat in the cavernous stadium, which is usually the home of more mundane groups like the Detroit Red Wings and professional boxers or wrestlers.

Pound Doors

• Teenagers battered on the doors and windows of Olympia, demanding admission more than two hours before the first of two shows was scheduled to start.

• A grim-faced battalion of more than 450 police officers got their marching orders from their equally serious superiors as crowds of fans chanted outside.

• Twelve girls were given first aid treatment during the matinee performance.

Less Hysteria

While the crowd, mostly young girls, attempted to shove their way through police lines outside Olympia before the first show, observers said the reaction to The Beatles was less hysterical than on their 1964 visit to Detroit.

Their two 30-minute performances here figure out to about $100,000 an hour onstage for the four Beatles—John Lennon, Paul McCartney, George Harrison, and Ringo Starr.

Crowds at the two shows included a number of boys sporting shoulder-length curls, a girl carrying a British flag, and teenagers in a varied assortment of English "Mod" fashions.

Screaming Success

Surprise hit of the show was a group titled The Remains. When they trooped onstage with long hair and offbeat clothes, the crowd screamed and began snapping pictures.

Commenting on the misunderstanding caused by his remark that The Beatles are more popular than Jesus Christ, Beatle John Lennon, in an interview with Leroy Aarons of the *Washington Post* said:

"

I can't express myself very well, that's my whole trouble....
I believe that what people call God is something in all of us....
But the record burning, that was the real shock, the physical burning. I couldn't go away knowing that I'd created another little piece of hate in the world. Especially with something as uncomplicated as people listening to records and dancing and playing and enjoying what The Beatles are....
If I said tomorrow I'm not going to play again, I still couldn't live in a place with somebody hating me for something irrational....
But that's the trouble with being truthful. You try to apply truth talk, although you have to be false sometimes because the whole thing is false in a way, like a game. But you hope sometime that if you're truthful with somebody, they'll stop all the plastic reaction and be truthful back and it'll be worth it. But everybody is playing the game, and sometimes I'm left naked and truthful with everybody biting me. It's disappointing.

"

The Beatles' press conference in Detroit.

17

George sings "If I Needed Someone" during the Detroit show.

■ One thing that people don't realize now is that back then it wasn't so easy to get tickets. There were no toll-free numbers, no credit cards, and very few interstate highways to zip along to other cities to see more concerts. Most people had to get tickets through the mail. I won two tickets from the Cunningham Drug Store Company, twenty-five words or less, why you liked their drug stores. We also bought a pair of tickets for $7 each—we gave the extra two tickets to the children of the parking lot attendant.

We saw lots of fans with Beatle decorations on their cars; one even had a huge model of a yellow submarine tied to the roof of their car. Our seats were about halfway back to the right of the stage in the stands. We were only a couple of seats away from one of the entry ramps. While The Beatles were on, we happened to look over, and there was Brian Epstein standing in the entry watching the concert!

It was too bad that the crowd's screaming was so loud that the songs were almost impossible to hear. The year before we had been on an exchange to England with our university and had seen the lads in concert in New Castle-on-Tyne. The concert was in a small city hall auditorium with about 2,000 people who actually listened to the songs and only screamed in between!

We decided to wait at the back entry to the arena after the concert to see if we could see The Beatles. There was a big crowd at first, but after half an hour there were only about fifty or sixty people, and we were all standing around talking about The Beatles and how great they were and which ones were the favorites (mine is John). The garage door finally opened and a huge bus came out. My friend and I ran back to our car across the street, got in, and followed the bus. Olympia is not in the best part of Detroit, so we were a bit apprehensive about where the bus was going and if we could find our way back since we lived in Ann Arbor. Surprisingly, we seemed to be the only ones doing this, and after about a mile, the bus pulled over and parked at the curb. We stopped behind it and wondered what to do now that we had our chance. We got out and walked to the side of the bus. One of the windows opened (can you imagine the excitement?!) and a member of The Cyrkle stuck his head out. We asked him if The Beatles were on the bus. He said they weren't, but would we like some popsicles?

So, we got back in our car, turned around, and headed home.

—*Sue Dolan*

REFLECT

REFLECT

I saw The Beatles in concert at Olympia Stadium, Detroit, 1966. It was right after the controversy over John stating that The Beatles were more popular than Jesus. While my friends and I were outside the stadium waiting for the second show to begin, a group of teens showed up with anti-Beatle signs. We chased them, seized the signs and destroyed them!

And yes, once inside, I was one of the many crying, hysterical girls, loving every minute of it! As difficult as it was to do, we decided to leave the building when we felt the show was nearing an end. We gathered out back where the Greyhound buses were parked and, sure enough, we got a glimpse of Paul waving to us as the bus drove away! What a thrill!

—*K.R.W.*

I was at that show also. My friends and I watched from behind the stage and nearly went nuts when John turned around and waved. After that they alternated throwing a wave and smile to the dedicated fans sitting behind the stage. I really treasure those memories.

—*Ted Graham*

I too saw the Fab Four in Detroit. I was up in the balcony and they looked like ants. I couldn't hear a thing because everyone was screaming so loud, especially me. I was fourteen at the time. . . . I just loved Paul. I even wore a black straight skirt and white blouse because I read in *Tiger Beat* that that was what he loved.

—*Lee Ann*

They played in Detroit, then took the Ohio Turnpike to play in Cleveland. Their bus stopped at the Vermilion (Ohio) Turnpike Plaza at 2 A.M., where I met them. Paul sang a shortened version of "Michelle" to me—a thirteen-year-old Michele. Imagine!

—*Michele*

This Week's Top Singles

These are the week's top 45 rpm singles, as selected by Detroit's top disc jockeys and the consensus of sales in the U.S. as reported by *Billboard*, international music recording news weekly.

#1 "Summer in the City"
Lovin' Spoonful

#2 "Li'l Red Riding Hood"
Sam the Sham

#3 "They're Coming to Take Me Away"
Napoleon XIV

#4 "Wild Thing"
The Troggs

#5 "Pied Piper"
Crispian St. Peters

#6 "I Saw Her Again"
The Mamas & Papas

#7 "Sunny"
Bobby Hebb

#8 "Mother's Little Helper"
The Rolling Stones

#9 "Somewhere My Love"
Ray Conniff

#10 "Sweet Pea"
Tommy Roe

CLEVELAND

■ TODAY

3,000 GIs land in Vietnam to bring the total number of U.S. troops to 291,000 in war effort.

Lunar Orbiter, traveling 3,800 mph started orbiting the moon. Information about the moon's gravitational pull (thought to be one-sixth that of the Earth's) will be relayed to computers at the Jet Propulsion Laboratory via three dish tracking antennas. Photographs of the moon's surface will be taken at 120 miles above the moon's equator.

The thirty-seven-day airline strike between union machinists and the airlines continues as union representatives walk out on negotiations.

Thousands of armed Communist troops parade through the streets of East Berlin to celebrate the fifth anniversary of the building of the Berlin Wall.

This year the average hourly wage of U.S. production workers was $2.56.

England defeated West Germany in the 1966 World Cup Finals.

Terminal Tower—Cleveland

Journal

Municipal Stadium—Cleveland

Sunday, August 14, 1966:

Woke up at 2:30 P.M.— it's a cold, damp, grey day.

We rode to Cleveland Municipal Stadium in the bus to play the first outdoor concert. The stadium is HUGE. We felt so strange being out on a baseball field! The stage is behind second base ... too far from the audience. The nearest person was at least 125 feet away from us. Felt like we had no contact with them at all. We could hardly see them, and they could hardly see us. What a drag! Hope the people felt differently about it. At least the weather warmed up some. Returned to the Statler Hilton right after our show. Didn't stay to see The Beatles play. There was some ruckus outside the stadium. I wanted to get out of there.

ON TOUR

with

THE BEATLES

by Judith Sims,
Editor, TeenSet Magazine

■ We arrived in Cleveland early in the morning, driving through the back entrance of the Cleveland Sheraton Hotel. There were no waiting crowds, apparently because no one knew when or how we were arriving. But, by ten o'clock in the morning, there was a large crowd. No press conference or taping session was scheduled, so we didn't see our four traveling companions. When nothing was scheduled, they stayed in their rooms like prisoners, listening to records, drawing or painting, watching television, sleeping, eating... except that they couldn't ever sleep too late because the fans outside were busy calling to them. Everywhere we went it was the same—the very fans who adored them enough to make them the biggest thing in the history of show biz are also the fans who make it impossible for them to enjoy their success. A Beatle can't show his head at a window without creating chaos; if one were to venture out to see the local sights, he might not return in one piece.

In spite of the gloomy Cleveland sky, there was no rain and the concert went as scheduled. There was a little matter of a riot with hundreds (some said thousands) of mobbing fans rushing the stage. The breakthrough occurred in the middle of their act, and the show had to be stopped because the police couldn't contain the hysterical fans. The boys just made it off the stage before it became crowded.

They escaped with no damage, just a close call. They waited in the trailer behind the stage for the riot to subside, but some of the press people were trapped outside in the midst of the brawl. It was a frightening first-hand experience, especially because the police kept mistaking me for one of the rioters!

Once the mob had quieted and returned to their seats, The Beatles insisted on continuing the show. That's what they were there for.

The last number of every show was "Long Tall Sally," and Paul always announced it as the last song and then tore into it for a screaming finale—but he didn't announce it as the last one in Cleveland. They plunged into the song, leapt from the stage (literally) into the waiting limousine, and the car practically launched into orbit. The rest of us acted as decoys in three other limousines, going through the expected exit. It was standard practice to lock all doors and keep all windows up—a practice that kept us healthy in Cleveland. The fans beat on our cars, jumped on the trunk, pulled at the doors—even when they could see there were no Beatles inside.

Back at the hotel, finally—a bit shaken—we learned that The Beatles' limo had had to crash through an obstacle because it couldn't afford to slow down. There was an estimated $400 damage to the car, and the limousine company refused to supply vehicles to carry us to the airport the next day. Several people spent a long night on the phone making transportation arrangements. Everyone got into the act somehow, and sure enough, the next morning a bus pulled up and we left with little panic. A few fans, who promised to remain calm and quiet, were allowed to watch The

While thousands rush the stage in Cleveland, one fan gets past police and manages to touch Ringo.

Hotel Sheraton—Cleveland

Journal

At the hotel The Remains and Ed Freeman had a long talk. We all decided it wasn't a very good show. While talking, we came to some amazing conclusions that we'd never accepted before:

1. We should record at lower volume
2. We should not go so physically into it on stage. Don't waste so much energy jumping around.

Then Norm went down to get some food. When he came back up, he said that everyone else on the tour was going to a party that Brian Epstein had invited them to. Norm thinks that everybody on the tour hates us. He said, "We're sure making enemies, man."

Beatles depart, but they weren't able to keep their promise. The Beatles got through all right, but Alfie fell down and cut his wrist and broke his glasses.

Before we leave Cleveland behind, I should mention the first party. There weren't a lot of people there, and it was rather quiet, but three Beatles showed up. John remained in his room, working on a device that made geometric patterns and designs. The gathering broke up fairly early; Ringo, who was the last Beatle to leave, had been sitting and chatting with a group of people. It was all very casual, very relaxed, and not the least bit wild. It wasn't anything like what I expected—but then, I'm not sure what I expected.

The Remains Set List

SLOOPY
WHY DO I CRY
DIDDY WAH
THANK YOU
DON'T LOOK BACK
I'M A MAN

CLEVELAND PLAIN DEALER

3,000 Fans Rush Stage, Force Beatles to Retreat

by Kenneth J. Moynihan

It wasn't much for the first ninety minutes or so. No one was picketing. No one seemed to care much about the disc jockeys and preliminary performers usurping the platform on second base.

The Ronettes were the last of four groups before The Beatles. They sat in the Indians' dugout in Cleveland Stadium awaiting their cue.

The Beatles arrived and the crowd was a typical Beatle crowd. Noisy. During the first two numbers, girls in the front rows climbed onto the wall separating them from the field.

It happened in the third number, and it happened first near home plate.

A boy decided to hop down into the area immediately in front of the stands, still separated from the infield and The Beatles by a snow fence and police.

A mob estimated at 3,000 followed him, and they stormed the fence. There was no chance of stopping them. Police lining the fence fell back to gather in front of the stage, then on the stage.

The Beatles kept singing. As police poked and pushed the fans away, they formed a cordon to whisk the singers backstage and into their trailer. That was guarded like the White House.

WIXY disc jockey, Al Gates, took the microphone, and kept it for the next half hour. Threats to call off the rest of the performance finally got the fans back into the stands.

As they filed off the field, the teenagers chattered excitedly. "Wow, we'll really make the news with this!"

"My mother's going to be frantic."

Gates, at the microphone, kept pleading. No need to pep up this crowd. He was upset, and his voice and manner showed it.

When The Beatles were finally back on, Gates was trembling. "I hope I'll never go through another thing like that," he said. "I lost 10 years off my life up there."

That would bring him to about thirty-four.

Before leaving the stage, Gates asked the crowd to stay away from the right field section of the park so that The Beatles could leave safely.

Soon, two black limousines moved toward that section. The Beatles finished without a comment about the mob scene, and then the four rich Englishmen were in a limousine dashing for left field. They made it as the WIXY disc jockeys tried to save the stage and the equipment left on it.

The demonstration was the first in The Beatles' current tour. Their concerts in Chicago and Detroit were quiet.

No cotton was issued for policemen's ears here, as it had been in Chicago Friday. Some solved the noise problem by inserting bullets instead.

Stadium officials said there was "extensive" damage to the baseball infield. Tickets for The Beatles were scaled from $3.00 to $5.50.

The Remains (left to right) N.D. Smart, Barry Tashian, Bill Briggs, and Vern Miller.

FANS REFLECT

REFLECT

■ My dad told me that The Beatles would be playing Cleveland's Municipal Stadium. He knew I wanted to see them, so he got tickets for my brother Dan (age sixteen) and me (age fourteen). They were the most expensive ones, costing $5.50 each.

The radio was playing as we drove to the stadium early that Sunday evening, August 14th. "Yellow Submarine" came on and the DJ said The Beatles might perform it at the concert. I knew that they could do it without effects, but that they probably wouldn't.

At the stadium my dad helped us find our seats and then left, saying he'd come back for us when it was over. Our seats were off to the right side. We settled in, took out the binoculars, and waited. There were more girls than boys in the audience, but there were many more than just a few boys. Revolver, which had been released only six days earlier, was being pumped into the stadium through enormous loudspeakers positioned in a half circle out on the field.

After awhile a limousine drove on to the field. It had to be them, I thought. The car stopped, the doors opened, The Beatles stepped out and the crowd gasped. The four were dressed in street clothes; later, on stage, they would wear identical suits. The Beatles looked around for a few seconds, and then went into their dressing room, which was a trailer next to the stage.

The show kicked off with The Remains, followed by The Ronettes (very ably backed by The Remains). They sang "Be My Baby." Next up was Bobby Hebb, who had a hit that summer with "Sunny." His backing was also supplied by The Remains. Bobby Hebb came after The Cyrkle, another of Brian Epstein's properties. They played and sang their hit, "Red Rubber Ball." As good as all of these acts were, they couldn't fully capture the attention of an audience so eager to see and hear The Beatles.

Then it started. Over the loudspeakers someone announced: "The Beatles!"

They ran out of the trailer and onto the stage. Without saying a word, John launched into "Rock 'N Roll Music." Girls all around us were screaming like we had all seen on TV. It sounded like a jet was taking off, but you could actually hear The Beatles through it.

I aimed my binoculars at John and marveled at how beak-like his nose looked as he crouched over the mic in a motionless stance, belting out the lyrics. They finished, there was a slight pause, and then came the distinctive opening chords of "She's a Woman."

The jet got louder, but I could still hear The Beatles through it. I noticed that the piano riff heard on the record was in this performance, played on guitar by George. While The Beatles played this song, I became aware of the fact that I

could not believe I was actually seeing and hearing them perform live. It seemed unreal.

It wasn't until they finished "She's a Woman" that any of The Beatles spoke to the crowd. Exactly who that was, and what was said, I can't remember. I do remember that when George did an introduction, he seemed annoyed by the noise the audience was making and waited for it to quiet down a bit before he would continue. The third song was "If I Needed Someone." George sang and played flawlessly. Speaking of George, at some point during the evening, he broke a string. While he replaced it, Paul told us we'd all have to wait a minute.

Next came "Day Tripper," the song that really worked the crowd into its wildest frenzy. About half-way into it, the fans mobbed The Beatles. Thousands of people ran down to the field and surrounded the stage. Some got onto the stage, but were thrown off by security guards. One girl climbed onto Ringo's drum stand. While all this was going on, The Beatles valiantly tried to finish the song, but couldn't, and ended up retreating into the trailer. An article in a Cleveland newspaper the next day reported the incident, but got the song wrong. I almost wrote a letter to set the record straight.

We didn't know what would happen next. Was it all over? After awhile, someone made the announcement that The Beatles would not finish the performance unless everybody returned to their seats. Eventually, everybody did sit down again, and The Beatles came back out. However, instead of playing the next scheduled number, "Baby's in Black," they skipped it and resumed the show with "I Feel Fine." Did they drop the song to make up for lost time, to punish the audience, or for some other reason? I don't know. In any case, "I Feel Fine"—one of my all time favorite Beatle songs—was sung and played perfectly. Next came "Yesterday." The stage was dark for this number except for a spotlight on Paul. George stood behind him and played the backing.

After the quiet "Yesterday," came a driving rendition of "I Wanna Be Your Man." It's a song I never liked very much, but it sounded great that night!

Next up was "Nowhere Man." John's voice cracked on the word "reee-al" at the very start of the song. This was one of the few flaws during the entire performance. All those jangling guitars sounded great on this number and George played another perfect solo, which even included the Ringo-delivered chime that comes after George's last lick.

After "Nowhere Man" The Beatles did "Paperback Writer," that summer's single. It, too, sounded perfect, except that at the end John and George could not manage all of the falsetto "pa-

perback writers" that end the song. Paul did sing his ending part, though.

After "Paperback Writer," Paul announced that they would be doing the "second to last" song of the evening. I thought that was an odd thing for him to say and didn't believe him. I figured it was going to be their last song and that Paul said what he did to prevent another mob scene when the audience realized that the performance was over. I was right, and they finished up with a rousing "Long Tall Sally." Apparently, most of the other stops on the tour ended with "I'm Down."

My dad reappeared in the middle of "Long Tall Sally" and watched for a while with us. We had to leave a little before the song ended to beat the crowds out of the stadium. I didn't see The Beatles leave the stage, but I later read that their limo got mobbed.

—*Jim Barrick*

The Cyrkle

■ TODAY

A U.S. helicopter gunship accidentally killed twenty-five civilians and injured eighty-two while striking at suspected Vietcong targets.

Birth Control pills, used by as many as six million American women, were given approval by the FDA, although research is still inadequate.

This year popular literature included: *In Cold Blood,* by Truman Capote; *The Crying of Lot 49,* by Thomas Pynchon; *The Last Picture Show,* by Larry McMurtry; *Tai-Pei,* by James Clavell; and *The Valley of the Dolls,* by Jacqueline Susann.

Medicare was begun to assist with medical expenses for persons over the age of sixty-five.

The first Black U.S. Senator, Edward Brooke, was elected in Massachusetts.

The Capitol Building

George and John pass time on the plane.

Journal

Monday, August 15, 1966:
Awoke at 9:30 A.M. After I showered, shaved, and packed, I met the others in the lobby at twelve o'clock high. We took the bus to the airport, but the plane wasn't there, so we had to wait a good hour. Meanwhile, The Beatles arrived on another bus.

I'm now onboard and we're in the air! American Airlines Charter. We're flying to Washington, D.C. A good lunch is served on board.

Soon, a number of people were standing in the aisle, socializing and smoking cigarettes. George smokes Peter Stuyvesants. Ringo likes to chew gum. Gum and lifesavers were in good supply from the stewardess.

I had a question about a percussion sound on Rubber Soul and thought this was a good opportunity to ask Ringo. "What's that tapping sound on 'I'm Looking Through You'?" I asked. He said, "Oh, I just tapped on a pack of matches with my finger."

That's great! Fantastic! I'm really happy to know that bit of inside information!

On Tour

with

The Beatles

*by Judith Sims,
Editor, TeenSet Magazine*

■ The next stop was Washington, D.C., but in many cases the plane rides to and from were just as much fun as the actual concert spot. Three of The Beatles circulated about the plane from time to time, but John usually remained seated. Several people came up to talk to him, which he did easily and pleasantly, but he wasn't his usual outgoing self, pointed out by others who had been on previous tours. John seemed friendly and attentive when speaking with someone, but he appeared troubled and reflective when he wasn't busy. I could be wrong, since I can't claim to be a John Lennon mind reader, but I may have seen more in his attitude than was really there. We (most of the press people) were all aware of John's difficult position

this year; so many people had taken verbal potshots at him that we were all a bit sensitive about anything relating to him. If John grinned, all was groovy. If John didn't grin, something must be troubling him. I asked him at one of the taping sessions if he realized he was a sort of barometer for the group in general. He said, very succinctly (and John can be very succinct), "No, I didn't. No idea." At a press conference later in the tour, John said, "When I look like I'm havin' a good time, I am. If I don't, I'm not, most likely."

The D.C. security in our fair capitol was pretty tight, as there were few people jamming the air-port or hotel. In Washington we pulled into the back entrance of the Shoreham Hotel where The Beatles and the rest of us had to trek through the lower depths and ride a creaky freight elevator to the lobby. That is, we went to the lobby for our room keys, but The Beatles don't have to do that sort of thing.

Washington was one of the few cities which did not have us routed through the nether re-gions to get to the concert site. We had a lovely ride through parks and past monuments. The Beat-les, at least, saw a goodly—and good—portion of our capitol.

All along the tour there were tough spots which were antici-

pated with a certain amount of dread on the part of the imme-diate Beatle group. One of those tough spots was Washington; supposedly the press would go after the boys and really dig in. The conference was held before the show in a hot stadium room, but the heat and humidity did little to dampen the enthusiasm of the aggressive Washington press. One of our tour party was heard to mumble, "It was like a bloody fan club meeting."

There were the usual dumb questions, as there were at every press conference, but it was gen-erally a positive, pro-Beatle thing. And, those are nice.

The concert there had one of

The Shoreham Hotel, Washington, D.C.

Ringo said he was interested in replacing his home stereo equipment, and asked me what I have at home. I told him: "Scott Amplifier, Garrard turntable, AR 2AX speakers." He said "Oh, that sounds good. Maybe I'll try that."

The Beatles had a little gut string guitar on board. George said, "Wanna try it?" and passed me the guitar. I played a few bars of "Freight Train." George called me a "Show off!"

Landed in Washington, D.C. The Beatles stayed at The Shoreham Hotel, and we went to The Willard Hotel.

I telephoned John Kurland (our manager). He was in high spirits about the tour so far. He said we have a full page ad in *Billboard* magazine and mentioned something about *Time* magazine next week, but wasn't specific.

the best sound systems and one of the largest crowds—over 30,000. The only incident, which brought a near heart-attack to our security men, occurred when a young boy came out of nowhere and leapt on the stage. He was quickly removed, but the crowd roared its approval anyway.

The getaway from the hotel the following day was a marvel of logistical planning. We all climbed aboard a waiting bus (we actually left through the front entrance, mind you) and took off, supposedly leaving The Beatles for a limousine or whatever. Instead, the bus circled around a few blocks and returned to another rear entrance, right up to some French doors. There were only two or three people watching, so the escape was effected without any problem. With our four Beatles firmly stashed in the back of the bus, we headed for Philadelphia.

Beatles Sneak in for Half-Hour Show: Barely a Screech From 32,164

The millionaire Beatles, a little longer in the tooth, but considerably better versed in theology since their last visit to town, entranced an audience of 32,164 subdued, orderly, young fans last night at D.C. Stadium.

Playing from a stand just back of second base in the huge arena, John, Paul, Ringo and George played eleven numbers in their half-hour share of the two-hour program.

The teenage crowd—a little longer in the tooth itself since The Beatles first burst on the world music scene in 1963—was even quiet enough to hear the lyrics. Only during Paul McCartney's rendition of "Yesterday" did the youngsters outdo themselves, sound-wise.

In a tight security blanket that included sixty Metropolitan policemen, 150 special police and a 600-foot-long snow fence placed strategically across the outfield, just one sixteen-year-old boy dared the undareable.

He burst past surprised policemen patrolling the left field foul line as the group launched "I Want to be Your Man," and managed to reach the stage before officers caught him.

He was handcuffed—amid cheers—and led off the field. Police later took him to the Fifth Precinct pending charges. He was identified as a College Park resident.

Three young girls made a brief try from near the right field dugout, but failed to get past the cordon of police.

Outside the Stadium, blocks away on 19th Street Southeast, and East Capitol Street, three lonely Prince George's County Ku Klux Klansmen, clad in red, white, and green robes, paraded for twenty minutes under close police survelliance.

The Klan appearance was the only obvious response to the first class controversy the famous four recently generated over Beatle John Lennon's remarks about Jesus and the fading popularity of Christianity.

Lennon touched on the controversy, gingerly, during a half-hour press conference held before the evening's performance in the Washington Senators' locker room.

Last night, asked if the resulting furor was "a tempest over nothing," Lennon replied, "It's something now. But, there aren't as many people seriously upset as I was led to believe."

He also said The Beatles didn't believe the remarks had cut into their attendance. "I don't think we're drawing any less than we expected," he added.

Colors Galore

The press conference, held under the tightest rules by officials of General Artists Corporation sponsoring The Beatles' fourteen-city American tour, was otherwise enlivened only by the quartet's splendid outfits.

Beatle Paul McCartney—on Saturday he jumped into the religious controversy in Chicago with, "We all deplore the fact that Christianity seems to be shrinking"—looked splendid in a mustard yellow sport jacket and a striped shirt.

Ringo Starr wore a lavender and white polka dot shirt with black velvet jacket. And George Harrison wore a buff colored sports outfit.

Lennon almost surfaced with another controversy when a reporter inquired if the group would think of entertaining the troops in Vietnam.

Responded Lennon: "I wouldn't want to go near Vietnam right now." The matter was dropped.

Earlier in the day, The Beatles' entourage flew into National Airport in a chartered American Airlines Electra. They landed in a northern corner of the field, to be met only by newsmen.

The party of sixty was then taken in six limousines, without police escort, to the Shoreham, where The Beatles were deposited. The rest went on to the Willard Hotel.

Girls Dispersed

About a dozen young girls—several of whom said they had been waiting at the hotel's service entrance since 7:00 A.M.—crowded around The Beatles' car as it stopped. Two District policemen and two Beatle security guards managed to disperse the youngsters, one of whom managed to have a good cry before the tussle was over.

The Beatles' Washington stop was the fourth on their whirlwind national tour. Crowds at their earlier appearances in Chicago and Detroit and Cleveland had all been smaller.

Last night's audience at the Stadium began to gather around 6 P.M.

Among them were Pat Corman and Andi Gibbs, both sixteen and both of Georgetown, Maryland. Long-time Beatle fans, they said last night's concert was the third they have attended —and they could remember to the hour, the date and time of two other Big Events in their young lives. Yesterday, they toured Washington hotels from early morning in a vain attempt to find their heroes. Lamented Pat: "We never thought of the Shoreham."

Armed with two gift teddy bears ("maybe we can bribe a policeman to throw them on

continued . . .

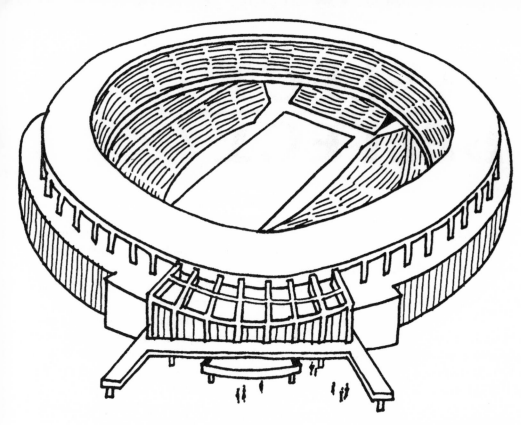

D.C. Stadium

32,164 Attend Concert

...continued

the stage for us") were Denise King of Springdale, Virginia and Peggy Kaye of Annandale, both 15. They also carried a large sign reading: "Paul We Luv Ya."

The Remains, a rock and roll group, opened the evening's performance. They were barely audible over the buzz of the crowd.

The sound system also plagued vocalist Bobby Hebb, as well as The Cyrkle, a young group on its way up as the first American quartet to be managed by The Beatles' own impresaria, Brian Epstein.

During The Remains' performance, two long limousines were driven onto the field to prepare the getaway for The Beatles. When the fabulous foursome concluded their concert, half a dozen teenage girls raced to the right field exit to meet the car. They lost.

Journal

I'm on the bus now, going to D.C. Stadium. We're on Pennsylvania Avenue with the Capitol directly ahead. It reminds me of the Arc de Triomphe, in Paris. On a whim, we pulled up to the White House gate and our tour leader, GAC's Sandy Scott, told the gatekeeper that we were The Beatles' entourage and would like to have a quick look in the White House, if possible. The answer was "No," so off we went on our way to the stadium.

This tour could mean so much to us. It's such a big opportunity.

I'm determined to be "Fantastic," "Brilliant," "Creative," "Dynamic," "Polished," "Confident"— that's what we gotta be!

The concert was groovy and we put on a great show. (If I do say so myself.) Back at the hotel, I met some friends in the lobby and we went across the street to Bassin's for a couple of drinks. Came home and went to sleep.

FANS REFLECT

REFLECT

■ I attended the August, 1966, Beatles concert at D.C. Stadium.

Being only eleven at the time and having screamed all the way through it, my memories are somewhat vague. I do remember having to buy the tickets through the mail, at $5.00 each for fifth row seats.

Somewhere, I still have my program and possibly my ticket stub.

I remember, most vividly, the opening riff of "If I Needed Someone," as "Yesterday" and "Today" (<u>Rubber Soul</u>-ed.) had just been released. To this day I get goosebumps when I hear that song.

Bobby Hebb ("Sunny") and The Cyrkle opened the show.

—*Jennifer DeBernardis*

This concert was one of the last on their last tour (*fourth out of fourteen—ed.*), and it was in what is now RFK Stadium in downtown Washington, D.C. They were one of about twelve other acts, including The Cyrkle ("Red Rubber Ball") and Bobby Hebb ("Sunny").

They played for about forty-five minutes to a very excited, flashbulb-happy, screaming crowd.

The most memorable part of the show came when someone, enraged by the then-recent John Lennon statement that The Beatles were more popular than Jesus Christ, broke past security, ran up to the stage and began pummeling John. In the tumult that followed, Ringo jumped down from his drum kit and pulled the attacker off. The crowd, needless to say, was taken aback by this, but the show went on.

—*Anonymous*

What We Were Watching

The Andy Griffith Show	Alfie	Frankie and Johnny
The Beverly Hillbillies	Born Free	Ghost in the Invisible Bikini
Bewitched	The Fortune Cookie	Hold On!
Bonanza	Georgy Girl	Out of Sight
Daktari	Harper	Paradise Hawaiian Style
Gomer Pyle, U.S.M.C.	Khartoum	Spinout
Green Acres	A Man for All Seasons	Wild, Wild Winter
The Jackie Gleason Show	The Professionals	
The Lucy Show	Who's Afraid of Virginia Woolf?	
The Red Skelton Hour		

Members of The Beatles' tour found ways to unwind and relax in between flights. Left to right are Tom Dawes of The Cyrkle, and Nedra Talley and cousin Elaine of The Ronettes.

PHILADELPHIA

■ TODAY

The *New York Herald Tribune* closed its offices forever, after being in business for 131 years.

The Board of Commissions held hearings on a proposed regulation that would make it illegal to possess hallucinogens including LSD, mescaline and peyote.

Quakers in New York announced their decision to encourage fellow Quakers to boycott all war efforts including payment of taxes. They urged the government to end the war in Vietnam immediately.

This year the Hare Krishna sect was founded by A.C. Bhaktivedanta Swami Prabhupada to teach devotion to the Hindu god Krishna.

The first endangered species list was issued by the U.S. Department of the Interior. It contained seventy-eight species.

Wilt Chamberlin, center for the Philadelphia 76ers, led the NBA in scoring with 2,649 points.

City Hall—Philadelphia

ENTER 7 | TERMINAL AVE.

ED | J | 1
Sec. | Row | Seat

BEATLES

PRESENTED AT

JOHN F.
KENNEDY
STADIUM

PHILA., PA.

AUG. 16, 1966
8:00 P. M.

UNDER AUSPICES

STEEL
PIER
MANAGEMENT

EST. PRICE | $4.76
CITY TAX | .24

TOTAL | $5.00

George, looking distinguished in his velvet suit, onstage in Philadelphia.

John F. Kennedy Stadium

Journal

Tuesday, August 16, 1966:
Enroute to Philadelphia:

Woke at 8 A.M. and took all our clothes to a dry cleaner in the D.C. ghetto.

We left the hotel about 2:15 P.M. enroute to Philadelphia by bus. Today will be a long day. Awoke in D.C. Tonight we'll sleep in Toronto, and do a show in Philadelphia in-between.

Arrived in Philly (JFK Stadium), and did a really good show. When The Beatles were on stage, the thunder and lightning seemed to augment the dramatic effect of their music. With all the flashbulbs going off, the flickering light made The Beatles look like they were stars in an old silent movie. The rain came barely seconds after the performance ended.

After the show, John Kurland met us backstage. He said he doesn't want us to talk to The Beatles— we should be above that— not on the level of the fans. But, I'm too much of a fan to resist talking to them.

ON TOUR

with

THE BEATLES

by Judith Sims,
Editor, *TeenSet Magazine*

■ As we approached Philly, our bus pulled over to the side of the highway and the four Beatles disappeared into a small panel truck —a florist's truck, no less. We learned that it was more for convenience than security—the bus couldn't fit inside the stadium.

The boys' dressing room in Philly was one of the few we saw from inside because a taping session was held there. John, Ringo, and George were seated on cots, Paul on a chair, and several fortunate young girls were dispensing sandwiches and soft drinks. It was during this session that I asked Ringo about his rings—or lack of same. He was wearing only two. "Congratulations," he laughed. "You're the first to notice it. I was wondering when somebody was going to ask." He said he had just taken them off about ten days before the tour, and would probably

put some of them back on when he returned, if he felt like it. He was wearing his wedding band (handed down from his grandfather) and a black opal ring gifted by the Jewelers of Australia.

The Philadelphia concert was one of several threatened by rain, which broke loose immediately after the show. It was a damp ride

to the airport for everyone—bus and flower truck together, but it was warm and secure once we got inside the plane.

At least the plane was secure while it was still on the ground. For most of us, the plane flights were times for mingling, relaxing, taking stock and comparing notes. For George Harrison, the flights

were an ordeal. "I just don't dig heights," he explained. It didn't help his height plight that our charter plane did not ride as smoothly as a jet. We hit some really rough weather more than once, which annoyed Paul (whose stomach is very easily upset anyway), and didn't exactly overjoy George.

Paul and George on the bus to Philadelphia.

Paul—Philadelphia

Journal

We got aboard the chartered AA Electra, Toronto bound. They served a very nice dinner of steak and baked potatoes and salad. I had a couple of drinks and talked to Harrison and Lennon.

I asked George if he ever had any trouble going through customs. The response: "Nobody wants to bust a Beatle for anything."

We talked about Indian classical music. He's really into it, and let Bill Briggs and me listen to a tape of Ravi Shankar playing the sitar through his headphones. It's really different than Western music. I like it!

I asked John about the use of the backwards tape on their song, "Rain." He said when they recorded the song it was too short. He said he took the tape home with him and played it backwards late one night and really loved the effect!

After going through customs, we arrived at the King Edward Hotel in Toronto at 2:30 A.M. Some fans were waiting by the door and, as I walked by, someone shouted, "Barry & The Remains!" It was amazing, surprising, and beautiful, so far from home!

FANS

■ "Ladies and Gentlemen... The Beatles!" the announcer shouted. JFK Stadium vibrated from the noise. It was Tuesday night, August 16, 1966. The weather was hot and muggy with high humidity. In the night sky, lightning flashed intermittently.

Pandemonium erupted from the wooden bench seats. Everywhere you looked you could see Beatles fans screaming, crying, smiling, and pointing. Necks stretched to catch a glimpse of the boys as they ran out onto the field toward the stage. One girl, wearing a sailor's hat with the brim pulled down around her head, left her seat and ran down the aisle toward the field in a frenzy of emotion. Another, in a print dress and sunglasses (at night), stood on her front row seat and proceeded to perform a beautiful dive of Olympic caliber into the tense arms of a policeman.

On the field were rows of policemen, spaced twenty yards between each row. Many had their hands over their ears. Behind the last row of policemen was a ten-foot high wood stockade fence which stretched in a semi-circle around the stage. Behind this barrier was a cluster of people—probably VIPs and the press.

Looming above this menagerie was the stage. Blue curtains parted slowly and revealed the familiar tiger-striped Ludwig drum kit. Below the riser rested the five-foot-high Vox super Beatle amplifiers—two to the left and one to the right. In front of the two end amps was a microphone and stand. Between them stood the announcer with a hand-held microphone.

The announcer lifted his arm and pointed to his right. The fans turned their heads to the left and peered. Excitement broke like a great wave over the stadium. Hearts beat fast with anticipation as we realized that, for a short time, The Beatles would perform live in front of us.

Suddenly, they appeared. They entered the field from a runway underneath the bleachers. Smiling and waving, they half-ran toward the stage. Flashbulbs exploded everywhere. The lightning increased in intensity, almost as if it wanted to join in on the fun. The noise from the fans began to build. However, one could pick out the individual cries from among the thousands.

"John, John, John!" "Paul, oh gosh, Paul!" "Georrrrrge!" "Ringooooo!"

Overall, the noise was one, big cry—something that you had to experience to appreciate.

The announcer, perhaps sensing danger, requested that the spotlights focus back on the stage. The field was plunged into darkness. The Beatles disappeared temporarily, and the noise level dropped a fraction. The crowd was getting its second wind, as the announcer piped up again: "Please do not stand on your seats or enter the playing field... Relax and enjoy yourselves... and now... The Beatles!"

REFLECT
REFLECT

There was thunder and lightning during the Philadelphia concert, but the rain held off until moments after The Beatles had finished.

From the left, John and Paul bounded onto the stage. Ringo rose above his drums from behind the riser. George was last. Each carried his instrument, Ringo his sticks.

They were dressed in green double-breasted suits with mustard yellow open-collared shirts. All wore black shoes which, on George, emphasized his white socks. John had a sheriff's badge pinned to his right lapel along with cherry red Granny sunglasses perched far down his nose.

"Hello, Philly," said Paul.

The crowd roared.

John and George tuned their guitars to each other. John played a tobacco-stained Epiphone, George used his black Gretsch, and Paul had the famous Hofner bass.

John looked to his right, smiled, nodded and turned to the crowd. He smacked out the four-beat intro to "Rock 'N Roll Music," and the greatest show on earth began!

There was very little banter between songs. At this stage in their career, The Beatles performed for about half an hour and called it a night, but, no one cared. The stadium rocked and rolled. This was an event, not a concert. This was something we could all brag about in the future—something to describe to our children and grandchildren.

"Rock 'N Roll Music" segued into "She's a Woman." There was a slight pause as George changed to a red-sunburst 12 string Ricken-backer guitar. He began the chords to a newer song, "If I Needed Someone." Afterwards, he switched back to the Gretsch and began "Day Tripper." This was followed by an oldie called "Baby's in Black." John and Paul waltzed around their sections of the stage during George's guitar solo. "I Feel Fine" was next with Paul doing the feedback intro. It was an odd sensation watching the group live, almost dream-like. You had to remind yourself that this was a live event and not the television or movies.

George introduced Paul, who began to sing "Yesterday." An eerie quiet permeated the crowd. *Everyone* was listening. An interesting note to this song is that it was performed by the whole group, with Paul playing bass.

Ringo's turn was next. After being introduced by Paul, he sang "I Wanna be your Man." I'll always remember Ringo, head shaking, a look of concentration on his face as he played, nodding acknowledgement when one of the others turned and said something to him.

This was followed in quick succession by

FANS REFLECT

REFLECT

"Nowhere Man" (with that beautiful three part harmony introduction) and "Paperback Writer."

The lightning had become overbearing. Rainclouds surrounded the stadium and threatened to burst at any minute.

Paul stepped up to the microphone. "Well, this will be our last tune." (Groans from the audience) "Sorry, but we don't want to be hit by lightning, you know. We hope you enjoyed the show," (the crowd cheered), "and we'll see you again, maybe next year. This last song is one that we've been doing forever, it seems. It's a Little Richard song called 'Long Tall Sally'."

They began the last song of the night and, as it turned out, the last live song they would ever perform in Philadelphia.

And then it was over. Quickly, John and Ringo left the stage, followed closely by a waving George. Paul remained. He bobbed his head to the crowd. He held his bass up by the neck in a final salute and, waving, disappeared behind the stage.

They entered a van parked at the back of the stage with lights flashing. It sped away with a police escort. And they were gone.

They were gone, but they left a lot of memories for me—memories that are still strong to this day and all for the ticket price of $3.00.

—*Jim Meehan*

I saw The Beatles live at Philadelphia's John F. Kennedy Stadium on August 16th, 1966. An ad announcing the concert appeared in the Sunday *Philadelphia Inquirer*. The ad said that tickets would go on sale May 7, at the Philadelphia Aquarama—that's right, an aquarium. The day of the ticket sale was a Saturday. I got up at 5 A.M and walked to the aquarium, which was about 10 blocks from my house. When I got to the place, there was a line of about 10-15 people. Tickets went on sale at 9 A.M. I bought 4 tickets at $5.50 a piece, with tax included. It cost me a total of 23.00 to get four tickets to see The Beatles. Unbelieveable!

Among our group of friends, anticipation was high. Ticket sales were dismal, at best. The concert never came close to selling out. JFK Stadium's seating capacity was about 105,000. The stage was placed on the 50 yard line, facing the horseshoe end, and seating was limited to 50,000. The final head count was somewhere around 20,000-22,000.

I had a friend who told me he didn't want to see them in 1966. He said he would catch them next year. Such luck! I didn't care about who or how many people showed up. The fact that I was going was good enough for me. *Anticipation was high all summer.*

By the time August 16th rolled around, we were all a nervous wreck.

On the day of the show we met up at my house and walked over to the stadium which was about a 10 minute walk from my house.

And believe me, magic was in the air. The Beatles had arrived in Philadelphia from Washington and came to the stadium in a flower truck.

The show was sponsored by George A. Habib, the owner and promoter of the world famous Steel Pier in Atlantic City, New Jersey.

If you have an original unused ticket from this show, look at the back and you will see a lineup of attractions for the Steel Pier that summer. The Stones, The Dave Clark Five, and The Animals all appeared in Atlantic City that summer.

The JFK show was hosted by Ed Hurst of local "Grady & Hurst" fame. With clouds gathering up ahead, the show began. The list of performers were Bobby Hebb, The Cyrkle, The Remains, and The Ronettes. Ronnie Spector told me recently that she was not a part of this show on the tour. Finally, at 9:33 P.M., The Beatles took the stage. They wore dark blue suits and, believe it or not, you could actually hear them. As memory allows, the show opened with "Rock 'N Roll Music" and ended with Paul screaming "Long Tall Sally." We were barely out of the stadium when the rains came. One of my friends took pictures with an instamatic camera. Years later, as I looked at the picture, I noticed that the policeman standing beneath John Lennon was the notorious Frank Rizzo, who later became Mayor of Philadelphia.

In subsequent years, I met all of The Beatles, but nothing will ever compare to the night when 20,000 people came together to celebrate the joy and magic of Beatlemania.

PS: I went to the stadium the next morning to watch them take the stage down, and I passed piles of Wednesday ticket stubs that were going to the city dumpster. What if?

—*Anthony P. Russo*

20,000 Greet Beatles and It's a Scream

by Rose DeWolf

While The Beatles were on stage at Kennedy Stadium on Tuesday night, lightning flashed and thunder underscored the electric guitars. But the rain politely waited until the British imports finished their last number and made a getaway before splashing down.

And, 20,000 youngsters, in long hair, mod outfits, and Beatle pins walked away, ecstatic, hoarse from screaming, and wet.

It wasn't really a big crowd (The mop-top quartet drew 32,500 in Washington), but it was LOUD.

It was a well-behaved crowd, if you don't count standing up and crowding in the aisles.

The Beatles go to a lot of trouble to keep their fans from smashing them to dust with love. They came into Philadelphia from Washington in a Greyhound bus; then, at the Walt Whitman Bridge, switched into a small florist truck. That took them unnoticed into the stadium.

Right after the concert, the little florist truck pulled up behind the bandstand. And, while their audience stood rooted to the spot, listening to the "Star Spangled Banner," the Liverpudlians jumped into the truck, were joined by two unmarked police cars, and zipped out an exit on the far side of the stadium. They went down to International Airport, where a chartered plane waited to fly them off to Toronto, Ontario.

When The Beatles came onstage, the flashbulbs started popping. Everybody seemed to have brought a camera. The flickering of the bulbs made the whole place look like an old-fashioned movie.

"If I'd known there was going to be this much light," cracked a stadium official, "we could have saved the city some electricity."

There were two funny things about this Beatles' concert—to anyone who has seen one in the past. First, you could hear them. (It may have been the sound system —very, very loud—but it may have been that the fans actually wanted to hear their idols.) And, second, there were BOYS there. About one-fifth of the audience was male.

The first throng of Beatle maniacs showed up at Kennedy Stadium at 6:30 A.M. They wandered around, hoping for a glimpse of the four most important people in the teenage world.

And a trio of ticketless-types even tried to cut their way through a hurricane fence behind the stadium, but were shooed away by the guards.

The real crowd began coming in at 6 P.M. and many brought gifts for the guys. There were hand-drawn paintings, signs, record albums... but, mostly, there seemed to be chains made out of chewing gum wrapprs.

"It's something you make to show you like a boy," explained Janet Young, thirteen of Abington, who came with an eighteen-foot length of spearmint wrappers for Beatle John Lennon.

While the fans tried desparately to get Stadium officials to tell them where The Beatles were hiding (no dice), the foursome stretched comfortably in a small room under the grandstand.

"It's like being in the calm eye of a hurricane," observed John.

Informal Interview

"It isn't boring at all," said Beatle Ringo Starr. "We have lots to do before a concert... dressing, tuning up the instruments."

The foursome granted informal interviews to six newsmen before the concert. They hadn't wanted a full-dress press conference. Their dress ran to a satin shirt and yellow sunglasses for John, tee-shirt for George Harrison, flowered sports shirt for Paul McCartney and a polka-dot shirt for Ringo.

George described their entry in a florist truck. "We came in disguised as a bouquet... or a wreath, depending on your viewpoint," he said.

Invade Korea

Other Beatle comments:

"We like each other more now than we ever did. We know each other so much better." (Ringo)

"Plans? We're going to form an Army, go through North Korea and take over Asia. Ha. We don't have any plans. It's better not to make them." (Paul)

"If the fans up there could get to us, they'd pull us apart. It's because they like us. And it's the thought that counts." (George)

TORONTO

August 17, 1966

Toronto waterfront—Toronto, Canada

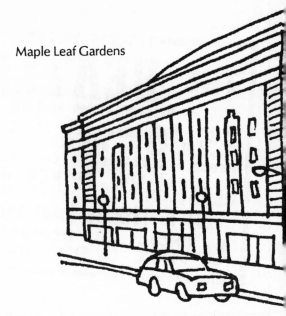

Maple Leaf Gardens

■ TODAY

As the airline strike continues, a contract giving the 35,400 members of the International Association of Machinists a $.56 cent-per-hour wage increase will be voted on Friday. The forty-day strike against Northwest, Trans World, Eastern, National and United Airlines seems to be nearing an end.

In Washington, a meeting of the House Committee on Un-American Activities led to seventeen arrests when shouts of "Get out of Vietnam" broke out from the witness stand. The committee opened hearings on a bill that would make it illegal for Americans to aid the Vietcong.

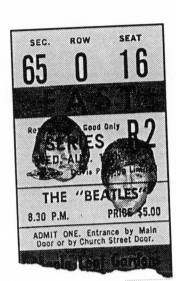

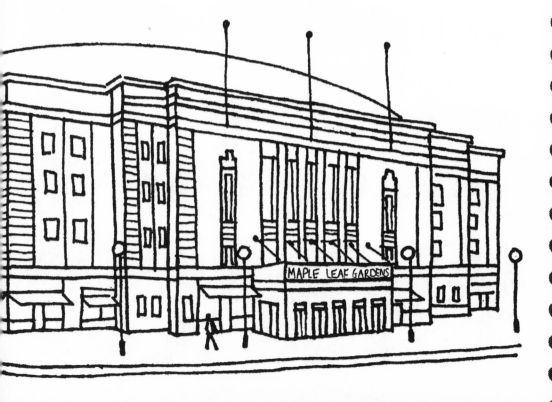

Journal

Wednesday, August 17, 1966:

We took a taxi cab to Maple Leaf Gardens at 2:30 P.M.

What a cool place!

The audience was up close and real near the stage. Great! After the baseball fields and stadiums, this was a relief. A chance for intimacy with the audience, and they were great. Yes... it was the best show we've done yet. I'm in the dressing room between shows. Two Columbia Records promotion men came in a few minutes ago and said that by tomorrow morning our record will be in every radio station in Canada. Ed Freeman went out to get a few things: hot dogs, gin and tonic, and guitar strings.

The second show was groovy. The sound was good— and the amplifiers too. I'm playing through a new Vox Super Beatle amp with two speaker cabinets, one on each side of the stage. At the show there was an incredible amount of screaming for *US*.

At the end of Bobby Hebb's act, N.D. ran out front and did three back flips across the stage. Show off!

Paul McCartney had a close call on stage tonight... someone threw a pair of scissors which narrowly missed his head. Why would a fan do something so idiotic? They say a Beatle fan will do anything to attract attention!

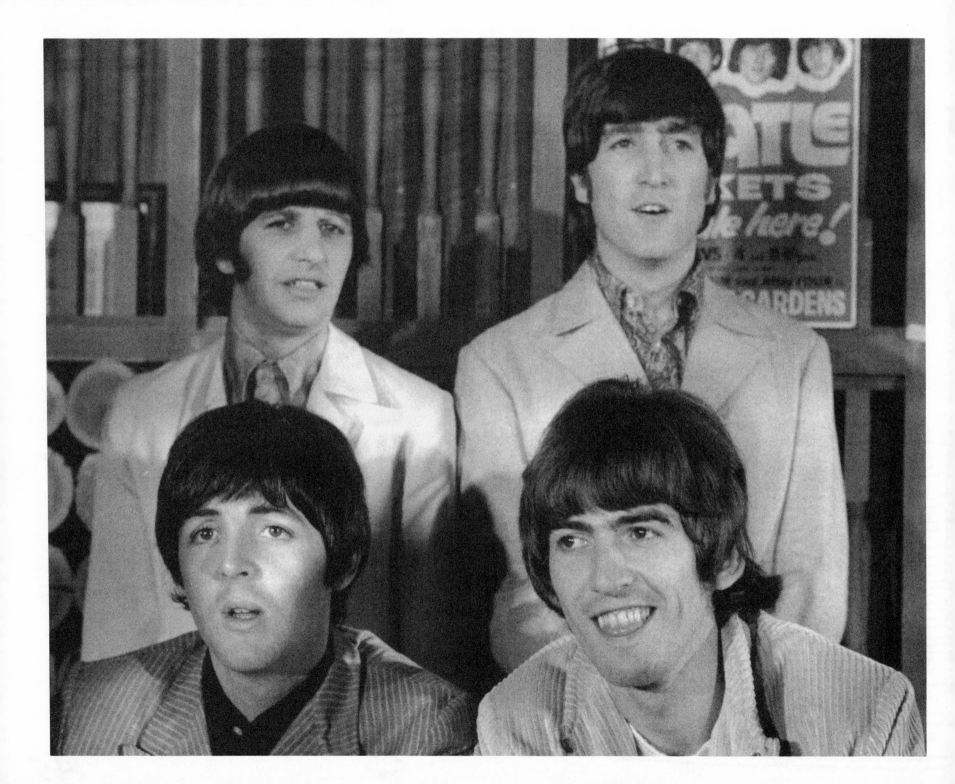

King Edward Hotel

Journal

George Harrison played my Epiphone guitar backstage tonight and asked if I was enjoying myself. George is a real guitarist— he has a feel for the classic styles of Segovia and Chet Atkins, too. He's a groove— a good guy, very natural and open.

I'm back at the hotel. The lobby is swarming with fans. Mostly for The Beatles, but some for The Remains. I like Toronto. It has beautiful architecture and a different atmosphere from the U.S. Two girls from French Quebec called my room and I spoke with one of them en francais depuis quelque temps. They're staying here in the hotel. These two girls are in the lobby and their names are Giselle and Loraine. I'm going down to talk to them for awhile.

Later, Ed, Vern, and I went up to The Beatles' suite. We watched TV for awhile with Ringo, John, and a few other people. The Beatles' suite looks like it's Christmas morning. Gifts everywhere, brightly wrapped with ribbons and bows— packages, stacks of letters and telegrams, big dolls, trays of food, rubber balls, a scooter, stuffed animals, and a Mickey Mouse tricycle. Pretty amazing scene!

ON TOUR

with

THE BEATLES

by Judith Sims,
Editor, TeenSet Magazine

■ From Philadelphia we headed north to Toronto, where we went through a quick customs line and had to declare our tape recorders (but not our cameras) before trundling onto another bus. The Beatles managed to elude the customs line, so they arrived at the King Edward Sheraton well in advance. There was a small get-together in their "living room" which adjoined their four bedrooms. Food and drink were spread out for their arrival, as was the case whenever it could be arranged. George was the only Beatle around while I was there, and he was busy discussing the Ike and Tina Turner recording of "River Deep, Mountain High." His opinion: "It's a perfect record from start to finish; you can't improve on it. I can't understand why it wasn't a hit in the States."

A great many people deserve a great deal of credit for making the tour work so smoothly and effectively; there were hangups, which are inevitable, but they were remarkably infrequent. Part of all the credit must go to the Toronto police forces. The two security men with our party said it was a pleasure being in Toronto because the police "did the job for us."

The two concerts at Maple Leaf Gardens were madness; the first was near capacity, the second, a sellout. These were two of only seven indoor shows, so the fans were closer and consequently threw things, usually flashbulbs, but also toys, candy—even shoes. George was hit in the face with a flying object, but he just grimaced and never missed a note. John later told some of us that they frequently collect goodies that are tossed at them. "If I see somethin' interestin', I'll ask Mal, 'Hey, Mal, get that or that.' He usually picks up most of it anyway."

There was a press conference in Toronto, too, for those who could get through the crushing mass of fans filling the corridors of the Gardens. Several of us had difficulty gaining admittance because the fans went a little wild and the police had to send everyone to an alternate entrance... but no one at the alternate entrance knew anything about our little red passes. It was frustrating at first, but we all made it eventually. The Toronto press had some pertinent and pointed questions which was the setting for one of the funnier lines of the tour. A man stood up and stated that The Beatles had been awarded the M.B.E. because of their assistance to the British economy; did they have any more plans for helping that economy? George shot back, "We could give our medals back!"

The second concert was pandemonium. There simply aren't enough superlative adjectives to stretch over an entire Beatle tour.

Back in the hotel after the show, Tony Barrow threw an impromptu party (no Beatles) which was the first occasion we had to get to know The Cyrkle, a very nice group and the first American group to be managed by Brian Epstein. The party lasted into the wee hours, until everyone was just too tired to lift another glass.

The following day we boarded that familiar bus, ran through customs again, and took off for Boston.

Presented by CHUM & AFTER FOUR

The BEATLES

are coming Wednesday!

You'll see them
THE CYRKLE
THE RONETTES
THE REMAINS
and BOBBY HEBB

AUG. 17th

TWO SHOWS
4 AND 8:30 P.M.

MAPLE LEAF GARDENS

TICKETS 5.50 - 5.00 - 4.00 BOX OFFICE OPEN 10 AM - 6 PM

Barry and Vern of The Remains.

CARTA D' ARMENIA
REP PROFUMARE GLI AMBIENTI
Brucia senza fiamma

Journal

Eventually everyone went home or went to bed except George's uncle. George asked us to hang out for a bit, so we waited until his uncle had gone home. Then we gathered in George's little bedroom, had a smoke and grooved for about an hour. George burned perfumed incense papers that came in a little red box from Italy. They were called "CARTA D' ARMENIA."

We played some guitar and listened to Ravi Shankar sitar tapes on a cassette tape player. I've never seen this kind of tape machine. It must be a new invention. It's a Phillips tape machine, and plays the smallest tapes I've ever seen.

We went into the living room, talked and played a Tim Hardin 45 rpm record that I brought along. Meanwhile, two of the roadies kept bringing these girls up to the suite, suggesting that George perhaps sleep with one of them. He wasn't interested and shook his head, no.

I went back "home" to room 1176. Briggs was there and he had some wine that Mike of The Cyrkle gave to him. Briggs said that there were fifteen phone calls and thirty-four people knocking on the door looking for autographs, etc. Finally went to sleep.

REFLECT
REFLECT

■ I saw The Beatles twice in Toronto at Maple Leaf Gardens, in 1965 and 1966. I was fourteen years old in 1965. I had never been to a concert of any kind, so this was a hell of a way to start. We had good seats on Paul's side of the stage. They only played for forty-five minutes, but it was great, even though we couldn't hear a thing. 1966 was the year that Lennon had made his Jesus comments, so he was very subdued and quiet.

This concert was also great. I remember that The Cyrkle also played. For both concerts there were numerous opening acts. Promoters hadn't figured out yet that The Beatles could sell the show on their own.

The Beatles were special. It is so sad that John is dead and any attempt to re-unite them now or ever will only be a big disappointment. I remember seeing the show *Beatlemania* on Broadway in New York City. I thought it would be great. They looked and sounded just like the real thing. But it had a real hollow feel to it. If you want a Beatles reunion, pull out your Beatle records (or CDs) and listen, because they ain't coming back.

—*Anonymous*

I went to see The Beatles in Maple Leaf Gardens in 1966. I enjoyed the show and went to the King Edward Hotel afterwards because I knew The Beatles were staying there. I milled about in the lobby for awhile until a tall man with blonde hair and glasses approached me and asked me if I wanted to meet The Beatles. I said I did, so he took me upstairs, right past the guards and into The Beatles' suite, which was on the 7th or 8th floor. I was nervous and almost fainted when we entered the living room of the suite and there were Ringo, John, and George watching television with some friends. Everyone was so friendly and normal; it was like sitting around with a group of friends at home. Ringo was funny—he kept making funny remarks about the movie on the telly.

I had a drink and talked with the man who brought me upstairs. His name was Mal and he was very kind to me. He took me over to one of the windows and we looked outside at all the people down in the street below. What a sight!

George had some relatives visiting him . . . an aunt and uncle, I believe. His uncle was a jolly man who liked to tip a few drinks of whiskey. George wasn't drinking. John seemed to enjoy

himself but was kind of quiet. I guess he was a little weary from touring so much and having to explain about that Jesus quote everyone kept nagging him about! Poor John.... When I think back now, it must have taken a lot of courage for him to face the whole of America, knowing the rage some of the religious fanatics were in!

John went to bed, and after awhile I went into another room with Mal and we talked until 2 A.M. It was time for bed, so I left The Beatles' suite and took a taxi home. My parents were not happy with me getting home so late. I was still a teenager then. They couldn't believe that I had been sitting around with The Beatles all evening—and my friends at school couldn't, either. I had a special photo of them that Mal gave me to prove that I had been there! I'll never forget it... and the memory of what good people The Beatles really seemed to be!

—*Sharon M.*

August 17, 1966 was absolutely the last time The Beatles appeared as a band in Canada.

We stayed on the 7th floor. The Beatles were on the 8th floor. If you were staying in the hotel you were allowed to walk on their floor anytime. We did not quite have the nerve to knock on doors. We did see an open door, and a suit like they wore that night was lying on the bed when we walked past. "Summer in the City" was playing in the room.

A bellhop told us he got all four of their autographs and sold them for $10. He thought he had made an immense profit.

The Beatles arrived at the King Edward at 3:00 A.M. There was an enormous crowd to greet them. It was so busy in the area that it looked more like a weekday than the middle of the night.

A small boy whose name was John Lennon was taken up to see The Beatle, John Lennon.

Ringo's drumming during "Paperback Writer" drew a special ovation from the audience.

Bo Diddley was playing at a small bar in Toronto while The Beatles were there.

—*Lance Blair*

■ TORONTO GLOBE AND MAIL ■

St. John crew treats 167 cases as Young fans pursue their idols

by Leslie Millin

Sweating, screaming teenagers surged through Maple Leaf Gardens yesterday for two performances by The Beatles that left the hucksters richer, the police wearier, and dozens of Beatle fans quite hysterical.

About 400 police struggled to prevent the swarming fans from injuring their idols or themselves, and managed to keep incidents to a minimum.

St. John ambulance workers said 167 teenagers were given first aid.

At yesterday afternoon's performance, youngsters in the audience tried to rush the cordon of police around the stage, but were held back. The evening audience contented itself with the traditional screaming.

The St. John Ambulance Society, which had 122 workers on the scene, said last night handled 117 cases inside the building and 50 outside. Fifteen persons were taken to the hospital, mostly for hysteria. One policeman suffered an injured ankle.

Some of those who had seen the afternoon show bought evening tickets—readily available—and joined the lineups snaking around the building.

Hucksters along the pavement sold Beatle pennants, photographs, and large buttons saying: "I still like the Beatles." Many of those heading for the show wore their own Beatle banners, however, like the sub-teenager with "Ringo" stenciled across the front of her jeans.

Once inside, Beatle fans fortified themselves with jellybeans and screamed half heartedly through the warm-up acts.

They were saving themselves for The Beatles. When the Mersey Beat specialists turned on their amplifiers, the crowd turned on.

Most of the audience showed considerable respect for the police lines, and usually sat down upon request from the officers.

Sidewalks were also blocked at the King Edward Hotel where The Beatles and their entourage spent the night before leaving at 2 P.M. today.

At the hotel, police guarded the steps, demanding to see room keys before allowing anyone through. Many Beatle fans had checked into the hotel, and schemed noisily in the halls about ways to get up to the eighth floor, taken over by The Beatles.

Many of the teenagers crowding the sidewalks outside the hotel and across the road from it clutched souvenir programs. Among them was a girl who had been carried by five policemen from the afternoon performance, flailing her feet and screaming: "I want to see Paul."

The chatter among the fans on the sidewalks—mostly from the 14,500 who saw the afternoon show, or the evening crowd of approximately 16,500—revolved around whether The Beatles would be back next year.

"I bloody well hope not," said a constable outside the hotel.

"They'll be back next year," said a tiny girl in bell-bottom pants. "Miracles do happen."

BOSTON

August 18, 1966

■ TODAY

The American space lab, Pioneer 7 began its orbit around the sun after a 404-day journey from the Earth. The space lab will monitor deadly bursts of radiation from the sun and measure solar gases and magnetic forces in deep space.

The Senate voted 3-1 to give the President authority to call up thousands of reservists and guardsmen for duty in Vietnam.

American war planes continued pounding targets in North Vietnam. Two planes were lost.

In Boston, a syndicate, including comedian Bob Hope, made an offer to buy the Boston Red Sox, but the offer was turned down by Red Sox Vice President Dick O'Connell.

This year *Webster's Third New International Dictionary* was published.

NBC television network debuted a new science fiction series, *Star Trek*.

Old State House—Boston

WELCOME HOME REMAINS
BOSTON LOVES YOU BEST!

The Beatles stayed at the Somerset Hotel for one night.

Somerset Hotel
BOSTON, MASS.

Journal

Thursday, August 18th, 1966
At 9:30 A.M. the phone started ringing and the knocking at the door started again. It was fans wanting autographs and looking for The Beatles.

I realized I'd left my wrap-around sunglasses in George's room last night. I called his room, but he had already gone.

After autographing our way out of the King Edward Hotel, we made it to the Toronto airport and onto the plane. When The Beatles arrived on the scene, they got out of their limo and walked toward the plane. I noticed George wearing two pairs of sunglasses! One of them was mine. When he came up the aisle on the plane he handed me my glasses.

We took off for Boston.

The Remains had a little welcoming party at Boston's Logan airport. Someone had a sign which read, "Welcome Home Remains!" Yesterday, there was a plane flying around Boston for five hours with a long banner, "Welcome Home Remains. Boston Loves You Best!" We took the limousine to the Hotel Bradford, a dump compared to the King Edward.

Suffolk Downs—Boston

Journal

The bus to take us to the show never arrived, so we took a limousine, and got to Suffolk Downs late. As we drove down the racetrack past the crowd, our limousine created a wave of pandemonium as we headed toward the stage. No doubt the crowd thought we were The Beatles.

Here we were in our hometown. It was disappointing that we couldn't hear our instruments very well. We went back to the hotel and ordered a steak dinner. That made me feel better. Slept.

The Remains

ON TOUR

with

THE BEATLES

*by Judith Sims,
Editor, TeenSet Magazine*

■ We stayed at the Somerset in Boston for one night only. Boston is memorable because it had the only racetrack that served as a concert site, complete with pond and swans in the back of the stage. The Suffolk Downs crowd first appeared to be a rough one, but fortunately, everything remained orderly. As orderly as a Beatle concert can get, that is.

In Boston a second young man made it onto the stage; he first informed one of the English disc jockeys that he had managed to get past the barriers and

hasty and forced exit from the stage.

The press party had to leave early to avoid the rush and to be in a position to act as decoys at every concert. We were always afraid that we would miss something important (like a riot) by leaving early, but, in most cases, the getaways were quite successful. We all made it to the Somerset unscathed, and spent a quiet evening. There were very few evenings that weren't quiet, come to think of it. None of us (Beatles included) ever seemed

Cynthia, usually cuts his hair, but since she wasn't available George did the honors. I can't tell you too much more about the Boston taping session because I was busy trying to take photographs which will, no doubt, turn out to be blanks. After that attempt, all photographers have my profound respect; anyone who can understand all those little dials and meters.... Fortunately Bob Bonis of GAC (who was with the tour on weekends) was snapping pictures just for the fun of it. I managed to con-

A typical crowd at a Beatles' concert.

guards to the stage area, and he further explained his intentions —to get on the stage and touch Paul. The disc jockey promptly interviewed him! After the interview, the boy went right ahead with his plans, causing great consternation among our beleaguered security men. Like the boy in D.C., this one also made a

to get enough sleep, but this was our work schedule, not our play time. It was tiring; it was fun; but, a wild fling it wasn't.

There was another taping session in Boston, short and informal, and John showed up with a shorter-than-we-can-ever-remember haircut, courtesy of George. He told us that his wife,

vince him that one could take photographs for fun and profit.

The Beatles played to more fans in 1966 than in 1965. Beatlemania—the most delightful affliction of modern times—is not exactly dead. It's growing!

The Beatles are silhouetted by the racetrack lights as they approach the stage at Suffolk Downs.

The Ronettes onstage with The Remains.

25,000 Teens Cheer Beatles at Suffolk

by Sara Davidson
Staff Reporter

George was uptight, scared. John kept his cool. Paul cooed, and Ringo sat high in limbo.

They played for just thirty minutes at Suffolk Downs, Thursday night. But, the germ of Beatlemania raged like an epidemic for more than five hours.

It transformed 25,000 fans into a wailing, shrieking wall of flesh that expanded and contracted, finally exploding in unhappy catharsis.

The girls—who made up ninety percent of the crowd—were crying and biting their nails as early as 6 P.M. when the race track gates were opened.

From 8:30 to 10:00 P.M., the collective nerves of the audience were pulled taut. They screamed, waved and jumped in the air each time they thought they spied a trace of The Beatles.

The Beatles played a round of old tunes, all of which were nearly inaudible because of the noise and tumult.

They wore forest green pants and jackets trimmed with emerald satin buttons and lapels.

Chartreuse pin-striped shirts with large floppy collars made the singers' skin seem ghostly pale.

George, the lead guitarist, seemed edgy, watching the fence-runners more than he watched the floodlit audience.

John smiled and played it casual on stage, eyes squinting ever so slightly, as if in communion with some spirit of amplified sound.

Paul (of the cherub face) tilted his chin heavenward and rolled his eyes. He timed his winks and waves to keep the girls in a suspended swoon.

Ringo Cheered

Ringo, sitting up high with his drums, wagged his head. His immitable holy fool's grin brought gasps of, "Ringo, Ringo" from the far reaches of the stands.

When the four struck up their eleventh and final number, a heavy-set young man in a green shirt suddenly leapt onto the stage, dug his hands into John Lennon's shoulders, then bounded over to Paul McCartney to pummel him on the back.

John and Paul just kept playing, but George Harrison, seeing the man heading for him, turned sideways and edged back and forth.

He was near the tip of the stage when two Beatle bodyguards rushed the attacker and drove him off the stage, into the clutches of six Boston policemen.

This touched off a volley of attacks by young girls, who sprinted toward the stage from every direction. The Beatles, not even pausing to bow, rushed into a black limousine and sped toward their sixth-floor quarters at the Somerset Hotel, reportedly $80,000 richer for their hard day's half-hour.

2nd Boston Visit

Boston was the sixth stop on a 14-city tour for the group. It is their second concert appearance in the Hub. The first was in September, 1964, when they filled Boston Gardens with a capacity crowd of 13,000.

Thursday's performance was sold out several weeks in advance. Tickets were listed at $4.75 and $5.75, but some girls reported paying as much as $10 for choice tickets.

Before the show began, Sharon Herrick, a seventeen-year-old from Portland, Maine, sat weeping in the first row, begging neighbors for aspirin. She sobbed out a story of paying $7 for tickets from an agent who guaranteed good seats.

"He put us in section one—miles down there. We couldn't see the backs of their heads. We couldn't even see the drums. So we moved here in the middle section and we don't care what happens. We're not moving."

As she shivered in a new spasm of tears, screams hit the air and the crowd rose as if on chorus. A black limousine pulled up behind the stage.

Kennedys Attend

Joseph Kennedy, thirteen-year-old son of Senator Robert Kennedy, leapt onto his chair to look. "What's everyone screaming for?" he said.

Kennedy and thirty-four friends and relatives had driven up from Hyannis Port to see The Beatles. They occupied two blocks of seats in the front sections.

Joe, who wore a wild print tie, which he said was "a joke," declared his favorite Beatle was John Lennon, adding, "He looks suave and debonair, and I like his hair. I don't think my parents would let me grow mine very long."

A leaflet circulating around the track declared in bold letters: "Beatles plan retirement." Young Kennedy frowned, "I don't believe it." A friend sitting next to him, fifteen-year-old, Chuck McDermott, agreed, "It would not be a sound economic investment to retire now."

Two blonde eighteen-year-olds from Somerville consulted their ouija board to verify the rumor. After shutting their eyes and moving the marker around the little board, Diane Turner exclaimed jubilantly, "They're not retiring. But, Paul's getting married to that actress Jane Asher on November 23."

A dying wail erupted from the next row. "That's not true. No, no, no. Don't believe it. Paul isn't going to get married," said Donna Provanzano, fourteen, of East Boston.

REFLECT

■ When I saw the Racetrack location on The Beatles schedule in *16* magazine, I asked a friend, who not only had his driving license but had his own car. My uncle had a beach resort near the Racetrack.

We asked his parents if we could drive from Connecticut to Massachusetts for a weekend at this resort and see The Beatles. His mother said okay!

The next step was to ask my relatives to try and get tickets. After bugging him for a week, my uncle called them. A few days later I heard that they had gotten tickets! Soon, two tickets to see The Beatles arrived in the mail. I couldn't believe my luck—two tickets, second row yet!!!

When we got to the concert and sat in our second row seats, I looked around in total anticipation... girls, girls and more girls. It must have been 9 to 1.

The set-up was odd, I thought. We were sitting in bleacher-type seats with a fence in front of us, then the racetrack, and, on the other side, maybe 50-75 feet away, was a wooden makeshift stage. We were really close.

DJs came and introduced groups such as The Remains and The Ronettes. While they were priming the crowd for The Beatles, I'll never forget looking to the left of the stage and seeing light reflecting off something shiny and moving. It was one of those *real* moments in

life. I noticed some figures, then John, then George, Paul, and Ringo. And, even though the noise grew to some incredible level, as they came into my full focus, bouncing up the stairs and onto the stage, I heard nothing—I froze. There they were. Holy shit, it's The Beatles, holy shit!

When I came back to some sort of consciousness, the crowd was wild and I picked up my 8mm movie camera and tried to film as the crowd shoved and screamed.

How cool they looked in those suits. I tried to memorize what I was feeling forever! And, I did. I think I even wrote down the song list. Then, in such a short time, it was over. A limo pulled up to the stage, they got in quickly, and the car pulled out on the track and drove right by us. And, for a fleeting second or two, there was John's face, looking out the window and waving. Again, holy shit! Girls were crying; it was such a weird feeling as they drove away.

I had the film developed, but never having used the camera before, I didn't know there was a filter over the lens. I still have these films; they're not very good, but I can see something in them no one else can!

—*Mike Sacchetti*

I was at the Suffolk Downs concert also. I was fourteen years old and went with my sister and a

friend. We had great seats in front of the fence. Besides the tickets only being four or five dollars, the show included Barry & The Remains, The Cyrkle, Bobby Hebb and the Shirells (I think). I remember driving home through the Sumner Tunnel, and everyone was singing Beatle songs with their windows rolled down!

—*J. Cox*

1966 Beatles concert at Suffolk Downs. I recall The Ronettes, Bobby Hebb, and "The Red Rubber Ball" songs. As soon as The Beatles came on, I no longer heard any music, just the screaming. I was actually frightened. Someone actually made it to the stage and kissed Paul and John. I was so jealous.

—*Nancy C.*

Saw The Beatles in '66 at Suffolk Downs Racetrack. Everyone had their eyes on the limos that pulled up, expecting the "Fab Four" to emerge. But, they had been in a little "shack" in the center of the unlit track all along.

—*Charles*

Hard to believe it's nearly three decades ago. We had just moved to the East Coast from Colorado—we'd only been in Massachussets for two days. I had purchased two sets of tickets. I was doing this to make sure I got at least one set of tickets. One I had gotten through some sort of mail ticket service that I'd seen advertised in *The New York Times*, and the other was from a friend of ours whose family lived in Weston, Massachusetts. I had two sets of tickets in hand, thinking I'd decide when I got there which was the better ticket to use.

I didn't know my way around at all because we were new and I was utterly flabbergasted by the rotaries and all the other features of Massachusetts traffic patterns that were unfamiliar to me. Having grown up in the West, where roads are straight and you have four-way stops, you don't have cars whizzing around and trying to hit one another. So, I was worried about getting there.

I was sure I couldn't wind my way through Boston. Looking at the map, it just looked like a clotted maze. So, I drove all the way up north on Route 128, and then came back down south from Marbelhead when I saw signs for Route 1. Somehow, I got to Suffolk Downs four or five hours ahead of time.

People were starting to gather. There was a short line already. I remember feeling a little awkward because I was not a teenager. I remember the book I brought with me—it was Dunleavy's *Ginger Man*. I tried to look studious and serious and preoccupied by the higher pursuits, while everyone around me was breaking down and acting like crazed Beatle fans. The first thing I did was to break down and act like a crazed Beatle fan when they finally let us in. I discovered that my first ticket was actually down on the ground. There were the bleachers or stadium seats, and then there were folding chairs set up in front of the stage. I had one of *those*, so I was feeling a little bit smug about that.

continued...

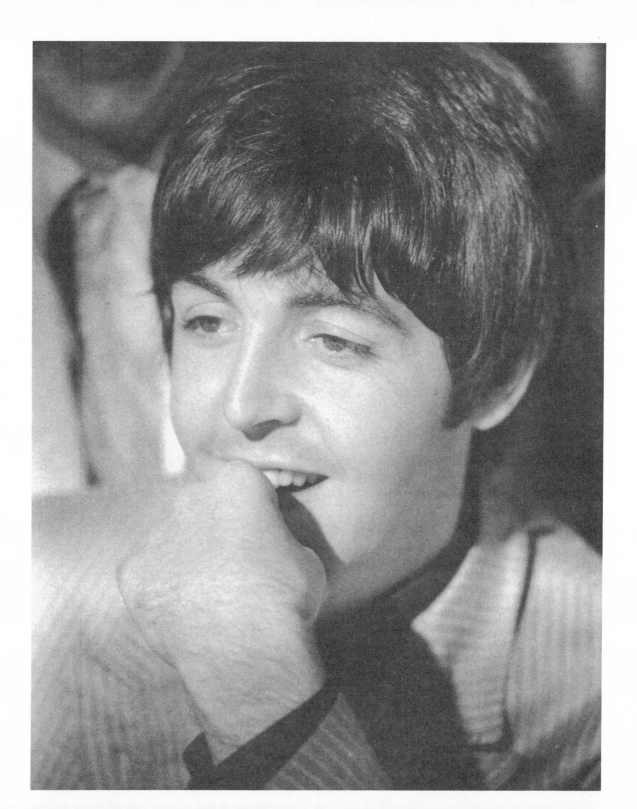

FANS REFLECT

REFLECT

...continued

I remember there were screams and shrieks at different intervals. I was sitting there reading my book. At one point, people screamed and someone said, ''I saw Ringo.'' Everyone started surging to the right and I surged with them. There was nothing, of course; people were out of their minds. They figured that one way or another, The Beatles would have to be sneaked past them, so everyone was being particularly alert.

It went from day to night and the crowd was getting larger and larger and people were getting more excited. I was struck by the fact that there were some families that had come. Some of the parents were sort of Beatle fans, too. When The Beatles actually came on, I saw mothers and daughters singing ''Yesterday'' together.

I remember a group came on and, while they played, the audience was surly and impatient. The DJ said, ''If you don't quiet down, The Beatles won't come on.'' But, no one believed that for a second. People were just shrieking. I was getting impatient for The Beatles to come on. During an opening set, there was a buzz in the audience and people were saying, ''The Kennedys have arrived.''

There was this whole bunch of Kennedys who came trooping in and sat in the very, very front row. They were getting the usual preferential treatment.

When the DJ finally shouted: ''The Beatles,'' people were just roaring. I was still holding forth on my seat in front of the stage, probably twelve to fourteen rows back, in the folding chairs. I could tell it was going to be out of control because people were standing on top of the chairs—chairs were being toppled over. I'm short and figured I wouldn't be able to hold my own in the melee. I didn't head for my other seat in the bleachers. That came sometime later. I certainly wouldn't have made a move when The Beatles were actually singing. I wouldn't have diverted my attention for even a moment. So, I shifted from the ground to the stadium before The Beatles came on.

They walked toward the stage from behind the scoreboard. John and Paul came from around the left side, and Ringo and George around from the right. You couldn't hear anything, just a roar.

John Lennon looked a little self-conscious. He was enjoying it. I always had

the feeling with John Lennon that his slightly surly edge was a way to compensate for an innate shyness or sense of the ridiculous. There was certainly something ridiculous about this mass hysteria.

I don't remember what the first song was because I couldn't hear much at all. That wasn't what it was all about anyway; it was the *experience* of being there.

I remember Ringo doing the head tossing bit and a couple of fans bolting and racing across the stage and trying to touch each of The Beatles in turn—John, and then George, and then Paul. People were cheering them on.

When Paul sang ''Yesterday,'' there wasn't actually a hush, but there were all these people singing along. That was quite powerful.

It ended very quickly, with the sense that this was something intense and communal. People were happy. They weren't growling. There wasn't a lot of the kind of quasi-radical posturing that I saw when I saw the Rolling Stones. I didn't see anyone drunk or having bad drug trips.

It was really a defining moment in popular culture. The Remains were bound to get lost in all of this, having the hopeless task of leading off The Beatles. That's like going on the stage to give a speech before Winston Churchill—not the ideal thing to do.

I wouldn't have missed it. I was determined to see The Beatles, and I'm really glad I did because that was their last tour and the last chance to see them. Now, when I mention that I saw The Beatles, people are a little awestruck. There is still a kind of powerful, almost religious, intense sanctity regarding them.

—*Jean Bethke Elshtain*

MEMPHIS

■ TODAY

The Senate approved an additional $58.2 billion for defense money for the Vietnam War.

Lunar Orbiter sent the first pictures of the back side of the moon to receivers on Earth.

Today in Little Rock, Arkansas, Major Homer Berry, a self-proclaimed rainmaker, was interviewed by a radio station during a heavy downpour. Berry said that he alone was responsible for the rainstorm, at which time the station was knocked off the air by a lightning bolt.

This year Masters and Johnson published *Human Sexual Response.*

Svetlana Alliluyeva, daughter of Soviet leader Joseph Stalin, defected to the United States.

Frank Sinatra won 1966 Grammy Awards for best record with *Strangers in the Night,* and best album for *A Man and His Music.*

Manuel Santan and Billie Jean King were singles champions at Wimbledon.

Beale Street—Memphis

Journal

Friday, August 19th, 1966:

Woke up at 7:30 A.M. and got on the bus at 9:45 to go to the airport.

The flight from Boston to Memphis was quieter than usual.

I sat across from John Lennon for a few minutes and asked him how he was doing. He said, "Ask me after Memphis." He did not need to explain.

We landed at a military airstrip. As we made our way to the Mid-South Coliseum in a city bus, we saw protestors along the roadside holding signs saying, "Beatles Go Home." We were instructed to crouch down below the window level for security. Today, instead of a limousine, the boys traveled in a Wells Fargo truck. We also heard that the Ku Klux Klan picketed one of the gates of the Coliseum. Because of death threats to The Beatles, security had been tripled.

There were two shows in Memphis— 4 P.M. and 8 P.M. The 4:00 show was delayed for an hour because of a bomb scare. The police had to check under the stage and around the Coliseum before they would open the doors. After all this excitement, it was a relief that the audience was more sedate than other cities have been.

Between shows, The Beatles got roast beef dinners, and the rest of us got Swiss cheese and ham sandwiches. At least the sandwiches were free!

ON TOUR

with

THE Beatles

■ The plane ride to the Southern city of Memphis, Tennessee wasn't exactly filled with fun and frolic, although several people were trying very hard to be casual about the whole thing. There was tension and undeniably worried frowns. As the plane landed, The Beatles began their familiar joshing with one another; one said, "Send John out first. He's the one they want." Another said, "Maybe we should just wear target motifs on our suits."

by Judith Sims,
Editor, TeenSet Magazine

Of course, Memphis was just great. From the moment we landed, we could tell that the people involved with The Beatles' concert (from motorcycle police escorts to bus drivers to fans) were outdoing themselves to make us feel welcome.

The first concert wasn't a capacity crowd, but they were very well-behaved; I couldn't believe it. There were no guards in front of the audience, only in front of the stage behind a wire fence. Girls were crying and screaming, but they were doing it in their seats.

There was a press conference between shows. The moment we had all been anticipating was upon us. We all imagined horrible things happening to John, spiteful questions and the like. It was a crowded, fan-filled conference and it went extremely well. Press Officer Tony Barrow had to insist, in a harried tone at one point, "No autographs at a press conference, please!" It was well over halfway through when someone mentioned "the" topic, and it was immediately greeted with groans, moans, and other signs of disgust. But, it was a mild question. Once it was over, The Beatles practically had to take flight to get out of there before the fan-type reporters could surround them.

Everyone started to relax after that. The worst was over and all was going so well. We started watching the second show with hardly a worry clouding our Beatlemaniac minds. We were shocked out of that reverie in the third number. Some idiot in the mezzanine had exploded a cherry bomb, which sounded far too much like a gunshot. It was several seconds (though it seemed like hours) before we started breathing again. The Beatles never missed a note.

When asked about it later, Paul simply said that when he heard it, his heart stopped, but he realized he was still standing and didn't feel anything. He looked at John and saw that he was still standing, so they all kept right on playing.

Throughout the tour, The Beatles never seemed to get shook about possible danger to themselves, while all around them people were having coronaries. Paul explained that they didn't worry about being hurt by their fans because they knew their fans just wanted to talk to them, touch them. It was only when there were thousands rushing the stage that it could become dangerous, but even then the whole thing was an adventure, not a frightening trauma. "When we were playin' in the old days, it was really dangerous," Paul said. "Guys would start fights, real fights, and we were in more danger then than we could be today."

Journal

During the 8 P.M. show, after the opening acts were finished, we assembled on the bus. Near the beginning of The Beatles' set, we heard what sounded like a gunshot. It was a real tense moment until we found out that it was only a cherry bomb. The Beatles were all right. In fact, their music never skipped a beat.

A few minutes later, we drove back to the plane and waited there. The Beatles followed directly. They seemed happy and relieved that the Memphis show was behind them and they were still in one piece!

We all began singing together and laughing.

Again, we had a chartered Electra from American Airlines. There was some time to wait for Mal Evans, Ed Freeman, and Mike Owens to bring the luggage and equipment to the plane. George asked me if I wanted a smoke. I said sure, so we got off the plane and walked out onto the grass. Smoking was prohibited onboard while the plane was on the ground. It was groovy just being out there on the field with the stars and the runway lights in the distance. Briggs and Neil Aspinall joined us. We didn't mention the cherry bomb incident, but we were all relieved it was nothing serious.

Bang Joins Shrieks In Beatle Show

The Beatles' beat got an unexpected bang last night as a cherry bomb thrown from the balcony of the Mid-South Coliseum caused minor injuries to four spectators.

A young boy and a young girl were being held by police.

The cherry bomb episode was the only serious mar of a day in which 20,128 persons heard the Liverpudlians bow to Dixie.

The musical performance of the long-haired Englishmen was hard to judge as the shrieks and screams of the paying guests almost drowned them out.

A near-sellout crowd of 12,539 shrieked through the evening performance, their cries echoing behind those of the 7,589 who attended the afternoon performance. Coliseum capacity was 13,050 for each show.

The total gate for the two shows was $110,704. The Beatles took $71,957.60 as their share of the Memphis sales under a contract with gave them sixty-five percent of the gate against a $50,000 guarantee.

The cherry bomb was thrown from the balcony into Section Z North just as The Beatles rocked into their third song in the night performance. Three young girls and a boy were treated in the Coliseum first-aid room. A companion identified one of the girls as Julie Wilson, sixteen, of 5197 Mason. Police refused to identify any of the injured.

Also withheld were the names of a sixteen-year-old boy and a fifteen-year-old girl pointed out by other spectators as the bomb throwers. Both denied the charge, but police found a sack with about twenty-five cherry bombs, and another with about twenty-five firecrackers in the girl's purse.

A number of other items, including half an apple and fragments of paper cups, were thrown onto the stage, but The Beatles smiled through it all. It appeared to be just the type of unrestrained welcome they are used to.

The ecstasy that greeted The Beatles was saved through an hour and fifty minutes of warm-up acts. But, it was nonstop from their entrance to their exit. Pandemonium between numbers was hardly less than during them.

The Beatles changed from the modish, dull-gray suits of the afternoon show, to dark green creations with chartreuse shirts for the night outing. John Lennon wore tinted glasses and looked a little like one who could stir up a world-wide reaction, as he did with his remark that The Beatles are more popular than Jesus.

The Beatles confirmed that last spring they planned to record an album in Memphis. It would have been Revolver, their newest.

McCartney noted that "little things, like money," intervened to prevent the recording session here. The Beatles' admiration for the guitar playing of Steve Cropper of Memphis was listed by Lennon as one reason they had hoped to record here.

Beatle fans from across the country filled most of the 6,000 hotel and motel rooms in Memphis yesterday.

"The Beatle fans are everywhere. We have been full in all motels and I have checked with other facilities, trying to help locate rooms for the visitors," said Mrs. Marion Brown, reservations director for Holiday Inns of America, Inc.

The Beatles left for Cincinnati by chartered plane at 12:11 A.M. today.

Mid-South Coliseum
—Memphis

George glances toward the camera during
The Beatles' evening performance
in Memphis.

Journal

When we were ready to take off, with all the equipment loaded, the stewardess came to the door and called us back to the plane. So, we ran up the stairs, buckled our seat belts, and we were airborne a moment later, Cincinnati bound.

I sat with John, George, and Ringo. We had dinner together— steak. John Lennon was in a good mood and looked especially relieved. It really blows my mind that I can sit and talk with The Beatles on the plane and feel perfectly relaxed and welcome. We talked about the fact that we'd be home in about ten days.

We landed at Cincinnati and were bussed to the Terrace Hilton. We checked in at 4 A.M. Went to the room with Ed. Tom Dawes and Mike Owen, from The Cyrkle, came to our room to talk. We've been on the go for twenty-three hours! Got to sleep at 5:45 A.M.

FANS REFLECT

REFLECT

■ Having grown up in Memphis, I was constantly exposed to both rock 'n roll and soul music. My friend, Judy, and I were eager to hear The Beatles.

I had a strong orientation towards R&B music. When I first heard The Beatles' version of Chuck Berry's "Rock & Roll Music," I was convinced that their heads were in the right place. It was evident they had a feel for R&B.

Anyway, we went to the afternoon show. They didn't fill the Mid-South Coliseum. We enjoyed Bobby Hebb, one of the openers who had a popular song, "Sunny."

When it was time for The Beatles to come on, they suddenly appeared from behind their amplifiers. Remember, this was the advent of the giant Vox amps. The audience was both surprised and amused by this. During the evening concert, someone threw a cherry bomb which sounded like a gun going off. A friend of mine happened to be watching Paul McCartney through binoculars. McCartney's face froze and his eyes darted about, but the band played on.

The lighting in the Coliseum was low, but somewhat illuminated, as opposed to dark with a spotlight on the band. In hindsight, I wonder if keeping the lights up was a way to help with crowd control. Years later, when Led Zepplin played there, the police told the Coliseum owner to turn the lights on to help subdue the crowd.

I never saw The Beatles live again.

—*Sohmer Hooker*

I was in the sixth grade when I went to see The Beatles with a group of girls. Someone's mother took us in a convertible and it was a big deal. When we got to the Coliseum, it was crowded. I couldn't hear anything. I couldn't understand what they were saying between songs. The thing that I remember the most was a firecracker pack that somebody threw at George's feet. There was a lot of screaming, and one of the girls that was with us fainted and had to be carried away.

One thing that was weird, now that I've been to other shows, is that I don't recall them having any help on stage; there weren't any techs. I remember Ringo's drums moving around, and he would get up and move them back. He had no help.

There was a rumor, before we went to the show, that they were at Elvis's house. I couldn't figure out why they would be there, because I thought Elvis was a greaser. Still, Elvis was great.

—*Pat MacMurray*

George and a member of The Remains share a soft drink before boarding the plane.

Revolver was released in the U.S. on August 8, 1966, just four days before the start of this '66 tour.

Rubber Soul was released in the U.S. on December 6, 1965.

CINCINNATI

The Ohio River—Cincinnati

■ TODAY

Russian cyclist Anatoli Derberashvili set a record as the first
person to ride a motorcycle to the
top of Mount Elbrus's 18,481 foot
peak, Europe's highest mountain.
Despite high winds and below
zero temperatures, he succeeded
after trying for two years. As

proof, Derberashvili left his motorcycle at the top and climbed
down on foot.

An earthquake rocked the moun-
tainous regions of Eastern Turkey
causing widespread damage as
seventeen villages in the province

of Anatolia were leveled. The estimated death toll could reach 3,000.

The airline strike ends after forty-
three days with a 2 to 1 vote ac-
cepting the wage increase. The
three-year contract will cost the
airlines $87 million.

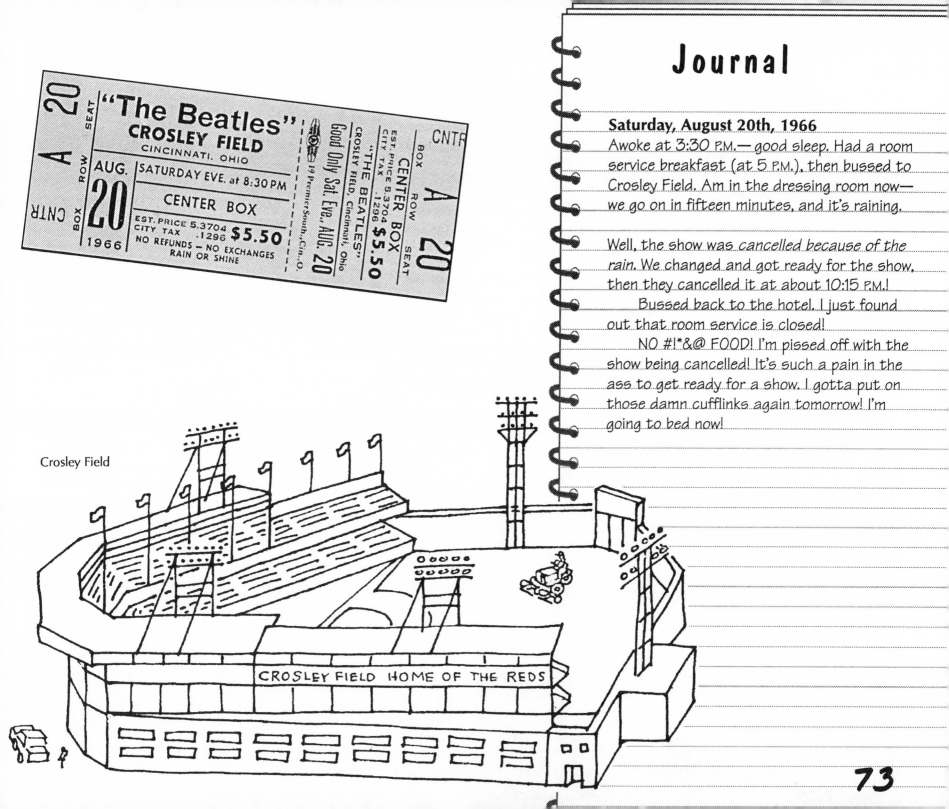

"The Beatles"
CROSLEY FIELD
CINCINNATI, OHIO

A 20 SEAT ROW BOX

CNTR

AUG. 20 1966

SATURDAY EVE. at 8:30 PM

CENTER BOX

EST. PRICE 5.3704 $5.50
CITY TAX .1296
NO REFUNDS — NO EXCHANGES
RAIN OR SHINE

CENTER BOX
BOX ROW SEAT
A 20

EST. PRICE 5.3704 $5.50
CITY TAX .1296

"THE BEATLES"
CROSLEY FIELD, Cincinnati, Ohio

Good Only Sat. Eve., AUG. 20

19 PremierSouth, Cin. O.

Crosley Field

Journal

Saturday, August 20th, 1966

Awoke at 3:30 P.M.— good sleep. Had a room service breakfast (at 5 P.M.), then bussed to Crosley Field. Am in the dressing room now— we go on in fifteen minutes, and it's raining.

Well, the show was cancelled because of the rain. We changed and got ready for the show, then they cancelled it at about 10:15 P.M.!

Bussed back to the hotel. I just found out that room service is closed!

NO #!*&@ FOOD! I'm pissed off with the show being cancelled! It's such a pain in the ass to get ready for a show. I gotta put on those damn cufflinks again tomorrow! I'm going to bed now!

CROSLEY FIELD HOME OF THE REDS

73

ON TOUR

with

THE BEATLES

by Judith Sims,
Editor, TeenSet Magazine

■ With Memphis behind us, much of the strain was gone. The bus ride to the airport (with The Beatles up front this time, still in stage suits) was one big sigh of relief and an unspoken compliment to Memphis. The Beatles changed clothes on the plane and we winged off for Cincinnati for another of our middle-of-the-night arrivals.

Time has not dimmed my impression of Cincinnati (which was shared by practically every member of the tour party). It was really pretty awful. Our hotel was a sort of residential hangout for older people in a not-too-groovy section of town. We arrived late at night and there was no room service, nor was there an all-night coffee shop in the hotel. There was a hamburger stand a few blocks away, but we were cautioned not to go there because it was a rough neighborhood. Our rooms were decorated in Early American Poor Taste, and the whole thing was a debacle. We did have one bright spot in the hotel, though, a private taping session with the boys in Brian Epstein's suite. Brian provided snacks and drinks.

The Beatles' stage at Crosley field as it appeared from the grandstand.

Vernon Manor—Cincinnati

The Saturday night concert was rained out; the promoter kept saying things like, "But it's never rained on a Saturday night before." There was no canopy over the stage in anticipation of rain, so the equipment was soaked. It isn't wise to plug in a wet amplifier.

But, The Beatles came to Cincinnati to give a concert, and they rearranged the whole itinerary so they could perform Sunday afternoon.

Sunday was hot and humid; by this time, there was a canopy over the stage, effectively blocking the upper seats from any view of Ringo. It wasn't a very large crowd for the performance—most of the kids were jammed into the corridor outside The Beatles' dressing room.

When The Beatles got on stage and hit the guitar strings, Paul made a face and yelled something at Malcolm, their equipment manager. It seems that his amplifier had been damaged in the rain and sounded like a "fuzz box." He couldn't force himself to smile during the entire show. He wasn't feeling well, and he felt terrible having to perform under bad conditions. Fans in Cincinnati got to see The Beatles, but they didn't see them at their best.

The Beatles escaped via limousine, while the rest of us plowed out in a bus, hot, sticky, and looking forward to that air conditioned plane. Goodbye, Cincinnati.

Neil Aspinall, center, and Alfie Bicknell, right, fight their way through an enthusiastic crowd to the stage, as fans strain to catch a glimpse of The Beatles and their entourage.

Journal

Sunday, August 21st, 1966

We got up at 7:30 A.M. and got to Crosley Field by 11:15 A.M., all checked out of the hotel. When I went out to the stage to tune my guitar, there was water in the guitar case from the rainstorm last night. Damn! A wet guitar. The show was at noon. It was sunny and hot, but very pleasant to be playing during the day under a blue sky. We had a canopy over the stage that kept the sun off of us, so it was cool. No electrical shocks from my guitar.

After the show, we went straight to the plane where I met George and Neil A. out on the tarmac. Time for another smoke before takeoff.

I'm on the plane now. We're landing in St. Louis for a show here and flying to New York afterwards, arriving at 3 A.M. What a long day, but it'll be groovy to go home and sleep in my own bed.

Double-Header With The Beatles

by Dale Stevens

If there are two unusual items in this world, they are The Beatles and Beatle fans.

The Beatles performed before about 12,000 young fans Sunday, noon, after a steady rain had forced cancellation of the original Saturday night plans.

About 15,000 people had arrived for the Saturday show. But, many of them were unable to return Sunday. Since the show did eventually go on, no refunds are likely for the thousands unable to come back.

Dino Santangelo and Steve Kirk, promoters of The Beatles' date here, weren't about to tote up the score by the time The Beatles flew out of Greater Cincinnati Airport, Sunday at 4 P.M. It will take several days to sort out the many complications caused by the last minute postponement of the concert.

But, the box office gross didn't quite reach the breakeven point by Saturday night. And, the extra financial obligations for the Sunday performance, which includes about $4,000 for police protection, might be steep.

The Beatles left Cincinnati with $60,000. That was their guarantee, reduced from the original $75,000 contract after John Lennon's controversial remarks about Christianity reportedly hurt ticket sales in several cities.

Sunday's show was as smooth as Saturday's affair was nightmarish. Veteran police officers asked me to compliment the young audience on its Sunday behavior.

There were, of course, the usual assortment of weeping girls after the show, a present-day phenomenon, brought on by the mass hysteria generated by the thrill of finally getting within a few hundred feet of their heroes.

The girls are as much a part of The Beatles' show as The Beatles—more, actually, since The Beatles were in sight barely half an hour.

They sang "Paperback Writer," "Yesterday," "Nowhere Man," and "Long Tall Sally," among others, and seemed to be having a good time.

The boys wore grey suits with plum striping (In the dressing room Saturday night, Paul McCartney had showed me his red belt and said it was our team colors, meaning the Redlegs.) and their trousers tapered into a slight bell-bottom effect.

Lennon had sunglasses of yellow hue. George Harrison featured the small, round granny glasses, and the only major difference between the four was their shoes.

McCartney wore boots; Harrison, moccasins; Lennon, a smart pair of red suedes; and Ringo had an ordinary pair of dress shoes.

After the show, they were hustled into an unmarked police cruiser which took off for the centerfield exit door. One girl eluded police to get out of the stands and through the door, but The Beatles were gone by this time, and she was greeted on the street by the police. "Oh, well," she said. "I tried."

The Beatles were preceded on stage by The Remains, The Cyrkle, Bobby Hebb and The Ronettes. The young Cyrkle boys were interesting, but all the acts were on far too long, and The Beatles' portion was far too short.

A standard star act does a forty-five-minute turn. This is routine in show business. And, for $60,000, the star should contribute even more. An hour of The Beatles would have been fair repayment for their audience.

The Saturday night rain-out was really something. It started pouring just before show time. The stage covering hadn't been installed, and before it could be, all electrical outlets were too soggy to permit the electric guitars to be used.

Still, I'm told, The Beatles were insisting that since the audience was getting wet, they were willing to get wet, too. But, the danger of electrocution was a major factor.

Another problem was getting permission to use Crosley Field again Sunday. John Murdough of the Redleg staff couldn't reach owner Bill DeWitt, but finally talked to Bill DeWitt, Jr.

At 10:25 P.M., after allowing The Beatles enough time to slip out of the park, the audience was told of the new plans.

I must say, they took it nicely, though there were tears from one group of girls who had to leave for camp today, and angry grumbling from out-of-towners who couldn't come back.

The patrons were admitted Sunday with their ticket stubs. Those who had lost them still managed to get in Sunday, when Santangelo and Kirk agreed to let all such claimants in fifteen minutes before showtime.

They figured the number of people who would sneak in that way would be insignificant compared to their service to the genuine ticket buyers.

The traffic jam Saturday night was monumental. It was tamer Sunday. Part of the problem was parents dropping their children off and returning to pick them up.

My backstage conversation with The Beatles will be carried on these pages within a day or two. Meanwhile, these final notes:

One teenage girl lost both contact lenses while jumping up and down during the Saturday excitement... John Lennon of The Beatles crooks his neck in rhythm, much like a Balinese dancer, as he performs....

Some of the girls yelled "traitor" and "fiend" at me after my story that The Beatles brushed off their fans . . . And, staff photographer Gordon Baer was given a ring by one of the girls to give to Ringo Starr—but The Beatles ignore most gifts. They get too many to keep.

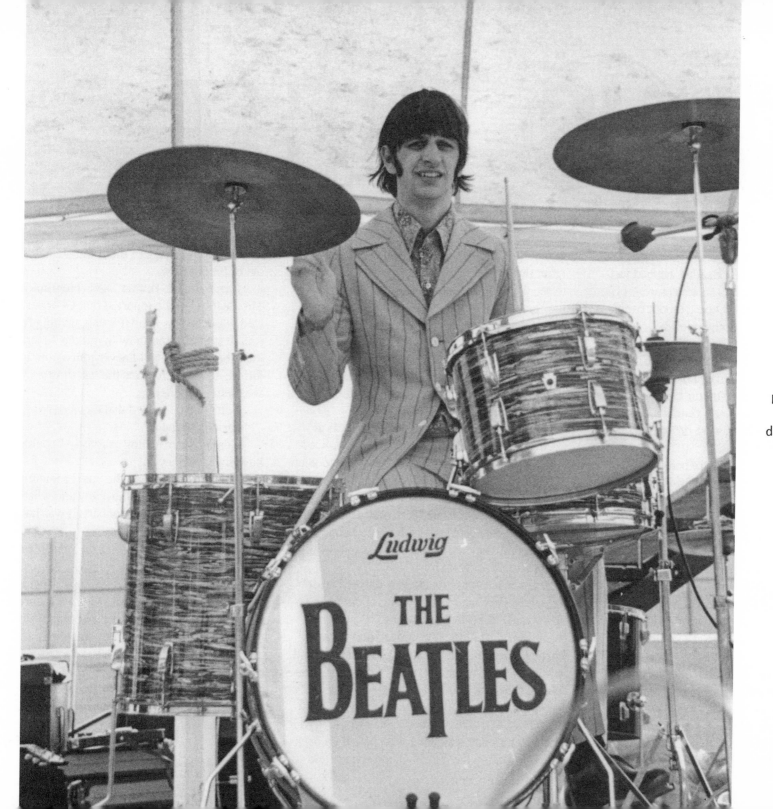

Ringo keeps the beat under the canopy during the noon show at Crosley Field.

FANS REFLECT
REFLECT

■ My best friend, Johnny, and I got tickets and made plans to go see The Beatles. He had just learned to drive and it was an adventure—off on our own so far away from home (about twenty miles). It seemed like another world.

That night it rained and finally they postponed the show until the next afternoon. Johnny couldn't make it the next day. I had just learned to drive and my parents wouldn't let me drive to the show, so my cousin and I caught a bus in downtown Hamilton and were dropped a few blocks from Crosley Field.

Where it was full the night before, it was about two-thirds full the next day. People had traveled long distances and could not come back the following day.

The Beatles were brought to the Stadium in a UPS van. I was standing on the second level, watching as the van came into the stadium. The doors were flung open and The Beatles made a mad dash of about fifteen feet to the dressing room. Someone jumped about fifteen feet off one of the roofs and, as best as I could tell, landed on Paul.

The show started and we hung around the dressing room to get a glimpse of them as they went to the field. As each act went on, we would run to see what we were missing on stage, then back to the cast iron fence that kept us from The Beatles. They passed about five feet away, and

as George passed, he said, "Hello Guv'nor." After they went by, we all ran out to the stands to see them hit the field. It wasn't a minute and they came out (running). Girls were screaming and reaching over the railings, trying to touch them. I thought it was all hype that girls would faint, but sure enough, they were dropping like flies. I guess what I remember most was how light brown their hair was and how pale they seemed.

The Beatles took the stage, which was at second base. The field was ringed with police. Most of them had put cotton in their ears to keep out the girls' screams. The policeman in front of us used two .38 caliber bullets as ear plugs. Surprisingly, you could hear them pretty well. This was the days before high-tech concert sound equipment. They used the stadium's public address system for sound.

The music was great—they played hit after hit, and before we knew it, it was about over. They said, "This is the last song," and a girl went over the dugout and dodged and weaved through the police and made it to the stage. And, just as Paul leaned down to touch her hand, the police caught her and dragged her off. The crowd booed the police and cheered the girl for her effort. We thought The Beatles would go out the way they came in, but a limo pulled up backstage and drove them through the center field

fence. My last image of them was Paul waving out of the window.

I had read the Hunter Davis biography on The Beatles and he reported that George realized while he was in a UPS van, waiting for the rain to stop at some show in middle America, that The Beatles would never tour again. Little did we all know that was the last time we would see them perform live.

Someone described that day as having "electricity in the air."

That was my feeling exactly—I couldn't have said it better.

On the way back on the bus, I remember people asking us about the show and what they sang. That was my first concert. It was hard to beat!

—*Reggie Mays*

I saw The Beatles at old Crosley Field in Cincinnati in 1966. It started to rain Saturday night, and we sat in the rain for hours watching them put up a tent. The show was then cancelled because they decided it was too dangerous to play electric instruments. So, we all had to come back the next day. It was worth it! I really couldn't see them or hear them, but just BEING near them was enough!

—*Sherry*

Looking back now, I realize that *I could not see nor hear anything —* but I was there! My dad refused to buy me a ticket for the concert. (He called them long hair freaks.) So, in order to buy the ticket, I went without lunch at school for weeks. $5.00! When I came to the States from Italy, I did not speak a word of English and, therefore, I had no friends. The Beatles were my only "friends." In fact, they helped me learn the English language just by listening to their records over and over again!

—*Anonymous*

I attended the Crosley Field concert. The concert was originally scheduled for a Saturday night, but because of rain, was rescheduled for the next afternoon. While ticket sales for the concert were pretty good, it was not a sell-out. It may have been that the backlash from the "Beatles are bigger than Jesus" controversy had an impact in this conservative area of the country.

The concert setup was awful, as would be expected for a stadium concert at that time. The stage was located around second base, meaning that even a front-row ticket would have been more than 100 feet away. I can recall a couple of the warm-up acts—The Cyrkle did "Red Rubber Ball," and Bobby Hebb did "Sunny." I seem to recall that there was a Motown "girl group," but I don't remember who it was.

The sound equipment was strictly low tech. I've often wondered if it was crude even for mid-60s standards. The P.A. system consisted of two rows of tiny Vox speaker columns set up along the base paths of the diamond. And, I don't believe they used monitor speakers on stage to hear themselves.

They came on to the predictable screams. As I recall, they wore grey suits with red pin stripes. John and George had their matching Epiphone guitars. As a concert, it was frankly pretty bad. They played for about forty minutes, and they didn't seem to enjoy any of it. As for the crowd, it seemed that the screams were obligatory.

But, of course, I couldn't have cared less about the music itself. For a twelve-year-old kid who idolized them, and who was inspired to play music himself, it was the experience of a lifetime. I kept the brown ticket stub in my wallet from then until the early 80s, when I somehow lost it. I'd give anything to have it back. But, I'll hold on to the memories forever!

—*Jim Carroll*

A young fan's excitement reaches a climax during The Beatles' performance.

Paul sings to the crowd at Crosley Field.

John Lennon wears granny glasses and plays his Epiphone Casino.

Paul squints in the noon sun while George wears sunglasses onstage at Sunday's noon show following the rain cancellation of the Saturday night concert.

The Ronettes onstage with Vern Miller, right, of The Remains.

■ TODAY

Airlines resumed operations as 101,000 airline employees went back to work. Thousands of travelers jammed the airports as 4,100 flights are back in the air.

More than 100 new Earth shocks continued to jolt eastern portions of Turkey. The known death toll at 2,300 continues to rise as rescue teams work in the remote areas.

The Reverend Martin Luther King and 500 demonstrators walked five miles in a march against housing discrimination today. They were met with jeers, rocks, firecrackers and bricks from the spectators lining the streets. Dr. King announced that he plans to march into Cicero (a section of Chicago) next Sunday with his civil rights demonstrators. The marchers will be violating a court injunction banning multiple marches.

This year the Tennesse Valley Authority began construction in Decatur, Alabama on a 1-million-kilowatt nuclear power plant. They estimate by 1972 there will be thirty additional plants in the United States, fifty-one more under construction, and seventy-two scheduled.

The Gateway Arch and skyline—St. Louis

Busch Stadium—St. Louis

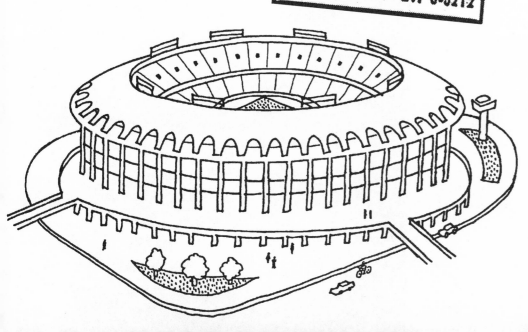

Journal

Sunday, August 21, 1966:

The ride from the airport took us past the new St. Louis Arch. Pretty groovy!

The show at Busch Stadium was wet. The stage was covered by a canopy, but everything was soggy. Our roadie, Ed Freeman was stationed at the main AC connection to the stage to watch the performers and un-plug the whole stage if anyone showed signs of an electrical shock. I mean, it was pouring down rain. Ed, who was pretty drenched him-self, had some towels wrapped around the ex-tension cord connection, and had a tight grip on it, eagle-eyeing the stage, ready to yank those cords apart before anyone was electro-cuted. Fortunately, the need never came up.

So far, the sound system at Busch Sta-dium was the toughest on the tour. The gig was hit-and-run. We used the park P.A. system— the same system used to announce who's at bat and on deck during ballgames. It had a monstrous delay. We were singing on stage behind second base, and the sound was coming out in the stands 150 feet away, two or three seconds later. There were no moni-tors on stage, and it was impossible to sing in time with the music. What I heard was an out-of-sync echo from the stands, and all I could do was close my ears and plow through the songs.

On Tour

with

THE BEATLES

by Judith Sims,
Editor, TeenSet Magazine

■ Sunday was a tight one; we no sooner left one concert arena than we found ourselves in the next— St. Louis. Brand new Busch Stadium was beautiful. We went to get something to eat, and when we returned, it was drizzling rain and The Beatles were already on the stage. This was the only concert we didn't actually watch from our next-to-the-stage vantage point. The show was almost over—at least The Beatles' portion. Because of the rain, The Beatles

went on in the middle, with The Cyrkle and The Ronettes finishing up the bill. We listened from the dressing room-limousine area, and didn't have to strain to know what was going on. There were kids surrounding the limousine area and blocking the exit. It was pretty obvious that we weren't going to get out very easily, let alone The Beatles.

It was confusion and waiting again. First, we waited around for a bus to show up backstage. Then, we waited in limousines. Then, we just waited. Finally, we were told that the bus was out in front of the stadium and we would have to brave the throngs to get to it. At this point, no one seemed to know exactly how The Beatles would get out through that crowd, but we followed orders and trudged through. The press didn't have much of a problem (not too many of us resembled The Beatles), but the supporting acts, who were to board the same bus, had a struggle. We were told later that The Beatles had escaped in a police car, through a back exit, with little trouble.

TOP: Despite the risk of electric shock on the wet stage, The Beatles play on at Busch Stadium.

RIGHT: A wet George Harrison during the show in St. Louis.

ENJOY THE BEATLES!!

BROUGHT TO ST. LOUIS BY

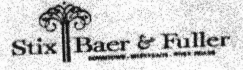

7up **and** Stix Baer & Fuller

DICK ESSER TICKET AGENCY

812 OLIVE STREET
ST. LOUIS, MO. — 63101

LAST CALL TONIGHT
STIX, BAER & FULLER
— SEVEN UP —
PRESENTS AT the new

BUSCH MEMORIAL STADIUM

St. Louis, Mo.

SUNDAY—AUG. 21—8 P.M.

THE BEATLES
Plus

THE CYRKLE—THE RONETTES

BOBBY HEBB

The Remains - Nick Charles, M.C.

Ticket prices: $4.50, $5.00, $5.50
tax incl. All seats reserved. Good
Seats Available.

TICKETS ON SALE
10 A.M. 'TIL SHOWTIME
AT STADIUM
TICKET WINDOW

—BI-STATE—
will extend its Redbird Express
for the Beatle concert from all
points for further bus information.
call PR 3-1120.

PRODUCED BY
REGAL SPORTS CORP

Journal

To top that off, The Beatles went on in the middle of the show. After The Beatles, The Cyrkle played, and then we had to go up on stage again to back The Ronettes, who closed the show. By this time, everyone was thoroughly soaked and wanted to go home. They had seen what they came to see— The Beatles— so the majority of our audience was on their feet, and moving as quickly as possible to the exits. It looked like a standing ovation, only everyone's back was turned!

By the time I got to New York, I was so damn tired, I just stayed at the Hotel Wellington with Ed.

STIX, BAER & FULLER
and SEVEN-UP present

AUGUST
21
1966
8:00 P.M.

ONE PERF.

BUSCH
MEMORIAL
STADIUM
ST. LOUIS, MO.

ADMISSION
$5.50
NO REFUNDS

LOGE
SEC 228
ROW 20
SEAT 17

— THE BEATLES —

Beatles Sing in the Rain for Wet, Enthusiastic Audience

by Robert K. Sanford

The Beatles played and sang eleven tunes in a light rainstorm last night before 23,143 paying spectators at Busch Memorial Stadium. Thousands of fans screamed for the music, thousands got wet from the rain, hundreds were terribly upset by it all, and a few dozen fainted.

The eleven tunes took about thirty minutes, and the rain was substantial at times. The fans sat in the rain and yelled. The Beatles were protected by a plastic canopy, but they also got damp. Their mop hairdos got damp, and so did the mop hairdos of their followers.

The members of the quartet told their press officer, Tony Barrow, that they did not mind playing in the rain, but were a bit apprehensive about the possibility of getting shocked by the wet electric amplifying equipment. But, once on stage, they grabbed the electric guitars and microphones fearlessly and attacked the music.

Disputes Talk of Decline

Barrow, The Beatles' press officer, said the alleged decline of The Beatles' popularity was mythical. "Beatle-knocking has become a new fad," he said.

Barrow said more American fans had gone to see The Beatles in the first half of their tour this year than had attended in the first half of last year's tour.

The fans at Busch Stadium got plenty of volume for their money, but the song lyrics were difficult to understand. The rain did not dampen the echo qualities of the stadium.

Jack Goggin, public address system operator, said the music was piped through more than 200 speakers in the structure. The system works well when performers speak distinctly, he said, but distinct enunciation is not a notable ingredient in rock 'n roll music.

Because it was thought that the rain might get worse, The Beatle performance was moved forward in the program, in the third position in five acts. The group that followed them, The Ronettes, was made up of girl singers.

When the girl singers appeared on stage, most of the girl spectators deserted their seats in the rain.

Some fans had come a long way for the show. A group of eighty-three had won an air trip from Denver in a radio station contest. Two girls from Memphis, who were dressed in boutique clothes (one wore a tailored glen plaid short skirt suit and hat, the other a dress of broad vertical stripes of green, orange and purple), said they had seen The Beatles in Memphis and were going to follow them to New York and try to get to talk to them. "Daddy's rich," one explained.

At the first aid station, two nurses treated twenty-five girls for minor injuries and ailments, the most common one being acute Beatle-mania.

"It's mild hysteria," said nurse Virginia Berger. "The symptoms are weeping, wailing and uncontrollable shaking. I tell them to sit down and cool off."

After The Beatles appeared, the nurses had about half a dozen young girls at a time in the station cooling off in shifts in the next hour.

The Beatles arrived in a chartered jet plane and were taken to the stadium in limousines. One limousine driver forgot to lock the back doors of the car after The Beatles got out and someone stole the rear floor mats.

After the show, The Beatles left in two police cars. About fifty young fans tried to get past police to touch the British singers. Some girls tried to scramble onto the police cars.

A seventeen-year-old girl from Creve Coeur managed to get hold of Ringo for a moment. Afterwards, she kept shouting, "I held him, I held him." She grabbed a reporter around the waist and said, "I held him like this!"

She jumped up and down, flailed her arms, then turned limp. Two policemen assisted her, holding her up by the arms, but they soon lost enthusiasm and let her down on the sidewalk. "She'll be all right," one said dryly.

Ringo sports a cap to protect him from the elements at Busch Stadium.

87

groov·y
groov·y (gr̄oo′ vē) *adjective*
groov·i·er, groov·i·est
Slang.
Very pleasing; wonderful.
groov′i·ness *noun*

John plays under the canopy
onstage in St. Louis.

FANS REFLECT

I was so excited because my dad got us sixth-row seats. However, when we arrived at the stadium, we found the seating was set up for football and our box seats were behind the stage! Luckily, we got into the press boxes. Those seats were a lot farther away, but we were the only dry ones when it started to rain!
—*Sharon*

Hello Beatle Fans. The St Louis' Beatles Fan Club is one year old. Anyone interested in joining can send $2.00 for a sample newsletter to:

St. Louis Beatles Fan Club
P.O. Box 190602
St. Louis, MO 63119

We are a not-for-profit incorporated group.

My aunt got my four brothers and me tickets to Busch Stadium. They cost $8.00 each. Recently, John had proclaimed that The Beatles were more popular than Jesus Christ. Probably true, but it didn't sit well with the old hard-line Catholics. Monsignor Ell, our pastor, announced that anyone attending the concert would be excommunicated! Well, my aunt wasn't about to throw $32 out the door. So, we went to the concert. Upon leaving, the Fab Four walked right to us; we got a personal autograph from each one. They were the greatest group of all time. I don't know what the autographs are worth, but there isn't enough money for me to part with them!
—*Anonymous*

In the summer of '66, the hippest thing one could be was in a rock 'n roll band. I was lucky enough to be the drummer in a band called U.S. Male in Robinson, Illinois. At sixteen years old, one must remember that The Beatles had arrived on the *Ed Sullivan* TV show. Around there, the Fab Four mopheads were scoffed at, and cussed at by those who hated long hair. But, they were generally loved by teenagers who were beginning to realize there really was something new in the world. When our band performed Beatles' songs to an assemblage of moist-handed adolescents, I remember thinking how their music made the "Cosmic Connection to my generation!" I was lucky enough, after a two-year wait, to get a ticket to a live concert 100 miles away in Busch Stadium.

Not having a car, I had to take a train, sleep overnight in the St. Louis train station, and walk to the stadium for the August 21, 1966, Sunday evening concert. Arriving at the stadium twelve hours before the concert, I was focused on only one thing. I was determined to get as close as possible and fully expected to get a picture when they arrived at Lambert Field. I began to examine the area around the stadium, when suddenly, a park district tractor came driving by with wagon attached. The wagon contained the dismantled wooden stage, which The Beatles would perform on! The work crew circled the stadium until it arrived at a maintenance entrance. Eureka! I watched the iron gates open as the tractor proceeded to second base on the stadium playing field.

Fans at the airport phoned the KXOX radio station to report that a limo had picked up The Beatles and was enroute to the stadium. By this time, the police had blocked off the street, and I was one of maybe a dozen people left well inside the police blockade.

The limo transporting The Beatles arrived within minutes and came to a complete stop in front of me. Limos in the sixties did not have tinted windows, and when Neil Aspinal, The Beatles' road manager, was spotted in the front seat, someone screamed out his name.

John Lennon, seated in back, leaned forward to see what all the commotion was, and when he did, I snapped his picture. The limo pulled forward and stopped, and all four Beatles stood behind the car and waved to those lucky fans, including myself.

The concert was performed in a light rain shower. The local police completely ringed the field for security. Technology was not as advanced in those days for such large outdoor stadium concerts. The boys played through their Vox amps on stage which were microphoned into the tiny twelve-inch stadium speakers. As predicted, the girls screamed throughout the forty-five-minute set, and it was impossible to hear. But, I am one of the lucky ones to see them live.
—*Steve Frye*

NEW YORK

August 23, 1966

■ TODAY

The Lunar Orbiter radioed the first good photographs of the far back side of the moon, taken at about 1,000 miles away. The area photographed showed dozens of large craters and hundreds of smaller craters in the area where astronauts hope to land in future missions.

The Food and Drug Administration has advised the government to restrict the use of antibiotics on food-producing animals. Penicillin, which is added to livestock feed, leaves a residue that could constitute a serious hazard for humans.

The Dow Jones Industrial Average fell 12.59 points to 792.03, the lowest since 1964.

This year New York City Transit raised its fares from $.15 to $.20.

Arial view of Manhattan—New York City

Journal

Monday, August 22, 1966:

Finally, a day off! I was busy in New York, meeting with our manager, John Kurland, visiting Manny's Music for some supplies and doing laundry. I invited George to come to my apartment to listen to records, but he said he didn't feel safe leaving the Warwick Hotel.

Tonight, I took my girlfriend, Valerie, over to meet The Beatles in the Hotel Warwick. It certainly was an elegant hotel. It was like going to visit royalty, and I felt privileged to escort her through the crowd of fans at the entrance, past the security guards, and on up to The Beatles' suite. As it turned out, John was the only Beatle we saw that evening.

For a while, we stayed in the living room, socializing with John, Alfie, and some girls. I looked out the window and saw the crowd of girls clustered around the hotel entrance, thirty floors below.... a Beatle's-eye view of the city— quite an unusual sight for a mere mortal.

After about an hour of small talk, we went into one of the bedrooms to play the *Tim Hardin 1* album I brought along. I thought John would like to hear "Reason to Believe," "Hang on to a Dream," and "Misty Roses." We sat on the floor by a small record player. John asked Alfie to find Brian

Journal

Epstein. Brian appeared almost immediately, dapper as usual. From his jacket pocket, he produced a gold cigarette case, opened it up and handed John a pre-rolled, filter-tipped joint. I've never seen such a perfectly rolled joint.

We played the record and listened closely, commenting between cuts. It was interesting to listen to an album with John Lennon; I heard it with new ears. Lennon really liked Tim Hardin's writing and the simplicity of production. I wish I could've given him a Remains album, but it won't be out until after the tour's over.

John told us he enjoyed the evening. He courteously thanked us for coming to visit and for bringing the album, which I left with him.

Valerie and I went back to our apartment and slept well.

Tuesday, August 23, 1966:
The limo picked up three of The Remains at the Hotel Wellington, and swung by to get me at my apartment around 3 P.M. We drove to Shea Stadium. A hot day, but the limo had AC…. or so we thought. The damn thing stalled out in the Shea Stadium parking lot, not 200 yards from the gate. We sat inside with no AC, the windows rolled up tight.

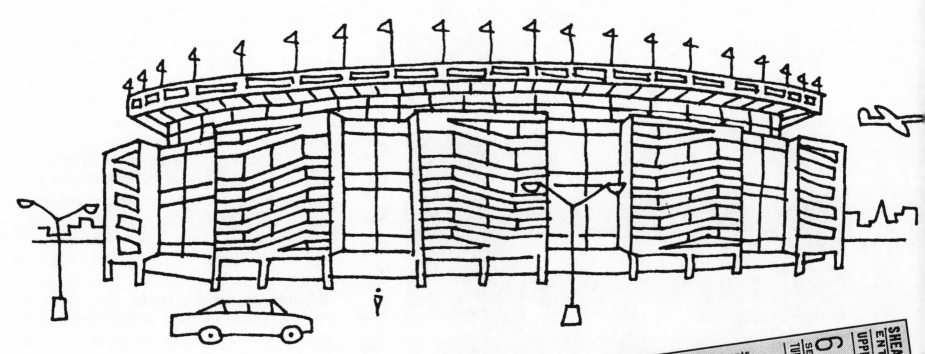

Shea Stadium

The Remains

Their first in-person appearances outside New England with the current Beatles tour— and the first reports are in!

'...They were the best of the curtain-raisers... (The Beatles) weren't any bigger...'

CHICAGO AMERICAN, Saturday, Aug.13th

Photo By Jerry Schatzberg

WATCH THEM TONIGHT!
NBC-TV's
Hullabaloo

SEE THEM TOMORROW
Shea Stadium,
New York City

HEAR THEM ON

A brand new hit!
'DON'T LOOK BACK'
5-10060

Journal

Girls swarmed on the limo like bees on a hive, so we couldn't get out. We were really starting to sweat. Half an hour of this and we almost suffocated. They finally got the limousine started. The limo got as close as possible to the door. Then, the police formed two lines between the car door and the entrance, and we made a dash for it! None of this would have happened if the fans had just noticed that we were not The Beatles. But, in the throes of Beatlemania, these distinctions were not made.

The Shea Stadium concert started a few minutes late. It's really strange to be out in front of 50,000 screaming fans with the stadium arc lights full on at night! The crowd was more restless and noisy than most, but at least some of the crowd paid attention to our set.

I played the electric 12-string that I got from Fender. We added my song, "Thank You," to the set, as John Kurland requested. It was good— maybe not fantastic, but groovy.

After the show, I got a ride back to Manhattan with a cat I met in the dressing room. Met Valerie at the Hotel Wellington. Finally slept.

ON TOUR

with

THE BEATLES

by Judith Sims,
Editor, TeenSet Magazine

■ We landed at La Guardia and limousined into New York to the Warwick. All those tall buildings... and all those aggressive teenagers. Avenue of the Americas was cordoned off, as were all streets surrounding the Warwick. Not just the hotel was guarded, but all points leading to it! Even so, our car was attacked. We barely made it to the front entrance without a bloody incident. And, then the guards wouldn't let us in! Wendy Hanson, Brian Epstein's personal assistant, summed it up by saying, "Well, that's it. We're once again secure against ourselves." After several minutes of looking harried and helpless, the guards were informed that we really were the tour party.

There was a press conference in New York—a very crowded, noisy, hectic affair held in the Warwick. It was immediately followed by a junior press conference, the first of its kind. The reporters were fans who had been selected at random by The Beatles Fan Club U.S.A. and WMCA radio. One hundred and fifty teenagers were given the opportunity of a lifetime to attend a press conference, take pictures, and ask questions. I expected excitement, but the whole scene almost got out of hand. They milled, they fretted, they giggled, they waited tautly, and when The Beatles finally made their appearance behind the microphoned table—chaos. It was like a concert in microcosm, with flashbulbs, screams, and rushing. Police lined the front table, stooping so the girls could photograph The Beatles. There was also a problem, because everyone wanted to take pictures and there was just so much room up front—Tony Barrow finally made them separate into two groups and take turns.

When the questioning began, things quieted down, and some intelligent things were said by fans and Beatles alike. I questioned George and Paul about their reactions to the junior press conference, and their

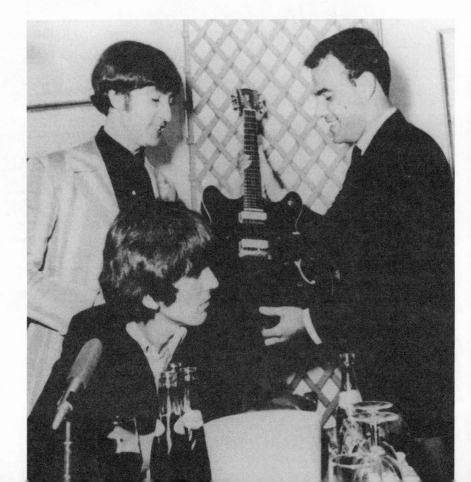

Mark Dronge of Guild Guitars presents a 12-string guitar to John during the New York press conference.

The Beatles field questions from reporters at the Warwick Hotel.

answers were almost identical. "We thought it was goin' to be a drag at first with all the screaming, but the questions were good. They're the fans; they ask what they want to know." George added, "I guess I'm gettin' old; I don't like noise. If they just wouldn't scream... but the questions were good."

The Shea Stadium concert was one of the most exciting (and packed) performances of the whole tour. Large signs were

more in evidence there (our favorite, "God bless you, John"). The show was apparently sponsored by a number of radio stations, as several DJs from several stations did the announcing. Contrary to a popular rumor, The Beatles did not arrive by helicopter. Their entrance wasn't so glamorous.

The press party tried to act as a decoy by running out to two limousines, but the kids knew better and just watched us run. The Beatles went out a different exit,

naturally, but they pulled into a way station not far from Shea right behind us. There ensued a comic opera sequence about who goes in what car, how do The Beatles get in, what to do... all because one limousine was overheating and wasn't too reliable. The Beatles vacated the limousine for an armored car.

Shea was madness, but New York's finest (police, that is) really were fine. And, there were clever barricades staggered four and

five deep in front of the stands. We watched the supporting acts from the dugout until we went out to the stage for The Beatles. It was always a thrill to be able to walk out to that stage while all those thousands of fans were eyeing us with envy and possibly hate.

We left Shea Stadium the way we came in—the limo for us, armored car for the boys. We went straight from the stadium to the airport, where we were hustled about like something from a Mr. Bond movie. We went to the terminal to wait for the regular commercial flight (not our charter, but a real flight with "outsiders" on board). There were so many people surrounding the loading area that we were spirited outside and around the back; we approached the plane from under the wing, no less. The Beatles and party had the entire first class section; the supporting acts were staying over in New York before flying to Seattle the next day. The Beatles were going to L.A. for a press conference and some time off before Seattle.

NEW YORK TIMES

The Beatles Bring Shea to a Wild Pitch of Hysteria

by Paul L. Montgomery

More than 45,000 teen-age girls—and a few anguished parents as well—rent the sultry Flushing Meadow air with shrieks and moans last night as The Beatles returned to Shea Stadium for their annual concert.

As usual, the noise was deafening, the music all but inaudible, the hysteria high and the money big—although not so big as in years past.

The attendance was about 10,000 shy of the Queens stadium's capacity, and at least one person—Sid Berstein, the tireless promoter—was a trifle disappointed. "But," said the sadfaced, round little man, "I think I knew it was coming."

Mr. Bernstein promoted each of The Beatles' four appearances in New York. Last year at Shea, each seat was filled and the gross was $304,000, from which the promoter made a tidy profit.

This year, with higher ticket prices, the gross was $292,000, and the four young men from Liverpool—George Harrison, John Lennon, Paul McCartney and Ringo Starr—get sixty-five percent of that. Mr. Bernstein said he didn't think there would be much left for him after expenses.

For their $189,000 last night, The Beatles were on the make-shift stage over second base for a half-hour. From the turmoil and the cacaphony there emerged snatches of "Yesterday," "Long Tall Sally," "Paperback Writer," "Nowhere Man," and five other numbers of The Beatles' own devising.

In a Wells Fargo Wagon

The Beatles arrived at the arc-lit stadium from their temporary digs at the Warwick Hotel, 54th Street and the Avenue of the Americas, at 7 P.M. They pulled up to the stadium in a red Wells Fargo truck, having transferred from their limousine at the old World's Fair grounds.

They had been in New York since early Monday morning, sheltered in their hotel suites from the swarm of teenagers seeking entrance. There they slept a lot, saw friends, examined goods brought to them by tradesmen of the city and, as is their habit, painted with tempera paints.

The Beatles rarely go out of their rooms when they are visiting America, and never travel with their wives while on tour.

The Beatles were preceded on stage by assorted disk jockeys and singing groups whose names appear to have been The Remains, The Cyrkle and The Ronettes. The stadium was strangley quiet, and the several hundred policemen on hand—including special patrolmen maintained by Mr. Bernstein at a cost of $15,000 —had little to do.

In the Mode

The vast majority of the audience was composed of teen-aged girls dressed in the latest mode. A sociologist would note that there were few Negroes among them. "That's true," Mr. Bernstein said. "There's a real split that way."

When The Beatles gained the field at 9:20 P.M., the shrieks began, building from a low moan to hurricane proportions. For the next half-hour, there was no let-up. Many girls cried, and a few waved articles of underclothing. The name Paul—the only unmarried Beatle—was on numerous lips.

The police, who had been standing by idly, suddenly found their hands full of struggling, weeping, hysterical teenagers. Several dozen girls were carried off, overcome. Others tried to rush the bandstand, but were apprehended.

When it was over, The Beatles left with a wave of the hand for Los Angeles, the next stop on their American tour. Mr. Bernstein said he believed the days of English rock 'n roll groups, with the possible exception of The Beatles, were numbered.

"From now on," he said, "It'll be all American. Remember what I said—I've never been wrong before."

To which fathers with pubescent daughters can only cry, "Mersey."

FANS REFLECT

REFLECT

■ 1966 was my favorite year. It was a wonderful year for music, wedged between folk-rock and the emerging sounds of psychedelica. That summer was a watershed year for garage band hits by groups with bizarre names like Question Mark and the Mysterians, Syndicate of Sound, and The Shadows of Knight. One group still reigned supreme—The Beatles, who turned the world on its ear once again with <u>Rubber Soul</u> and <u>Revolver</u>. Two days after my sixteenth birthday I saw them perform at Shea Stadium.

I was a veteran of the 1965 Beatles concert at Shea, but that experience, exciting as it was, paled in comparison to their 1966 performance. I had field-level seats and could actually see them without the aid of binoculars. There were about 5,000 fewer people in attendance than in 1965. Also, there were more male fans at Shea in 1966. These factors resulted in less noise. Although the conditions were still less than ideal, I could hear The Beatles sing and play.

That is my fondest memory of the 1966 concert, being able to see and hear them, unlike a year earlier as I sat in the upper deck, trying to figure out what song they were singing, or if they were playing anything at all. Three decades have passed since August 23, 1966, but I can still recall watching and listening in amazement as The Beatles did "Nowhere Man," "If I Needed Someone," and "Day Tripper," intro-

ducing the latter as their "Number One hit from 1965."

At times, I did use my handy pair of opera glasses and observed each Beatle individually. At one point, I thought John Lennon was waving at me, only to realize he was acknowledging a poster behind me that congratulated the Lennons (John and Cynthia) on their fourth wedding anniversary. Although we now know The Beatles were sick and tired of performing live, the smiles on their faces indicated they were having fun that evening. I know I did!

—*Marc A. Catone*

I'm a veteran of both Shea concerts: August 15, 1965 and August 23, 1966. The second concert happened to be on John and Cynthia's anniversary, so I decided to make a banner for them and hang it at the concert. Imagine my dad's reaction when the paint leaked through the sheet, and the message "Happy 4th Anniversary, John and Cynthia" was now on the driveway!

Both concerts were a thrill for me, as I was a major fan (still am). The second time ('66) I could actually hear some of the music. I was so pleased that I got the braces off my teeth the day before the '66 concert in case Paul looked my way. I was miles from the man, but when he did glance my way, I happily flashed him my new-found teeth.

When I gave birth to my first-born, I used a little picture of McCartney as my focal point during LaMaze breathing! And, I named my second child (and first son), Paul. Do I have a tolerant husband, or what? I've seen McCartney twice at Giants Stadium, a few miles from my New Jersey home, and he was fabulous. But, nothing will ever top those concerts at Shea!

One of my most moving experiences was going to Central Park, to mourn John's death, with one of the girls with whom I went with to both Shea concerts. I don't know at which event I cried the hardest.

—*Anonymous*

I saw them in 1966 at Shea Stadium with a fellow Nebraska friend. We were in seventh heaven! Here we were, seventeen year old Beatlemaniacs, getting to experience our heroes. It was sheer pandemonium. Everyone was in ecstacy. I remember a young man two rows in front of us screaming, "George, I love you, George." We thought that was pretty funny. The police formed several rows around the stage, and people still got through. It was something I'll never forget.

—*John R.*

■ TODAY

The unmanned Apollo Moonship splashed down in the Pacific Ocean after orbiting the earth. The next capsule will carry three astronauts into Earth's orbit in December.

Lunar Orbiter sends the first photograph of the Earth at 240,000 miles away taken from the vicinity of the moon.

This year popular songs included "Alice's Restaurant," by Arlo Guthrie; "Scarborough Fair," by Simon and Garfunkel; "Good Vibrations," by the Beach Boys; and "Mello Yellow," by Scottish singer, Donovan (Leitch).

The Space Needle, built for the 1962 World's Fair, and Mt. Ranier decorate the Seattle skyline.

The Beatles deplane in Seattle.

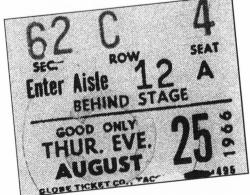

Journal

Wednesday, August 24th, 1966:
Got up early to run some errands in New York before meeting the tour at the Wellington hotel at 9:45 A.M. Bid farewell to Valerie and got on a plane to Seattle, a commercial jet this time. Had a nice flight.

We just landed and we're on our way into the city.

Seattle is a nice-looking city. The old buildings are really well-maintained out here. Arrived at the Benjamin Franklin Hotel in the afternoon.

N.D., Vern, Mike Owen, and I decided to take a look around the city. We jumped into a cab and went down to the waterfront. We got on a ferry and rode thirty-five minutes to Winslow, an island off Seattle. What a beautiful place it was.... forest, trees, woods, and some real nice people.

For $1.04 we rented an open-sided picnic shelter on the beach. We had a bonfire and marshmallows. It got pretty cold, so we took the last ferry back to Seattle at 11 P.M. Returned to the hotel and I slept very well.

ON TOUR

with

THE BEATLES

*by Judith Sims,
Editor, TeenSet Magazine*

■ Seattle was gray and overcast, but presented a delightful sky-and-sea-line as we drove by the waterfront and up to the Center where the World's Fair had been set up. The Seattle Center was a lovely new facility, and once again we were allotted our own little press room, which came in handy for another private taping session. The Beatles' dressing room was just across the hall, and the press conference was held between shows in the hall itself.

The first show was another blast, except that one of the microphones kept swinging around and wouldn't stay put. Paul finally gave up and went where the microphone went, sometimes singing with his back to the audience, sometimes on tiptoe... the hazards of show biz!

The big highlight of the Seattle trip was the rumor that Paul would meet Jane Asher in Seattle and marry her there. Hotel reservations had been made, a cake had been ordered—all in the name of a mysterious Mr. Bartholomew—and the whole thing was one big mistake. But, the rumor drew a lot of attention to the Seattle performance, and gave the Seattle press several questions for the conference.

The Edgewater Hotel on Elliott Bay where The Beatles stayed while in Seattle.

Seattle Center

Journal

Thursday, August 25th, 1966
Showday in Seattle:
Valerie called this morning with good news—
we got a "pick hit" in *Variety!* We did two
shows at the Seattle Coliseum, a groovy hall
with a good sound system. The fans stayed
in their seats and were very well-behaved
during the first show.

Later, at the sold-out evening show,
there was a wilder mood in the Coliseum. Toward the end of The Beatles' portion, a small
group of kids tried to break through the
police line and rush the stage. They didn't
make it.

Enroute to Los Angeles:
Just boarded the plane, an aging charter, for
L.A., and we're waiting for the equipment. It's
night, and George and I went outside again
for our nightly meeting of the "tarmac
smokers' club."

This plane was really old. It looked bad
and sounded worse. To make matters worse,
aviation fuel had been spilled on the runway.
As we began to taxi, one of the engines back-
fired and N.D. freaked out. He stood up in the
aisle and demanded to be let off the plane.
He said he had a fear of flying and had prem-
onitions before and was always right. To my
amazement, the pilot actually turned the

Beatles Storm Seattle

by Rolf Stromberg

Amid security arrangements that were practically war-like, The Beatles of Liverpool, Knights of the British Empire, convulsed an afternoon audience of 8,200 and an evening sell-out of 14,382 entranced youngsters Thursday at the Seattle Coliseum.

By every conveyance, the teenagers assaulted the Seattle Center: Monorail, car, Seattle Transit and on foot they came, often looking as bedraggled as tattered pioneers who had barely crested the Cascades.

Many of the girls were apprehensive. During the day, a report had spread that Beatle Paul McCartney would wed British actress Jane Asher secretly after the evening performance. This The Beatles expressly denied. McCartney jibed at the report:

"Tonight? Yeah. I'm not confirming it. It's a joke. How did it all start, does anybody know?" Asked whether he knew Miss Asher, McCartney winked and twisted his jaw; "Yeah. I've heard of her." Harrison added, "If she comes in tonight, we'll miss her. We're going out tonight."

The Beatles, who slipped quietly out of Hollywood early Thursday to land in Seattle aboard a chartered jetliner at 1:40 P.M., were sealed off from any contact with the crowd. Inside, the Coliseum was roped off; the low, wooded walls used for hockey were placed in front of the bandstand and a cordon of police behind red chairs blocked any entry. But, there was no need. The youngsters heeded admonitions to remain seated and keep the aisles clear.

For a half an hour of singing at each of two performances, The Beatles took $73,717.81 from Seattle in the biggest single day's gross ever in entertainment history here, according to Zollie M. Volchok of Northwest Releasing, the sponsoring agent. The total gross income reached $118,071, as The Beatles earned a percentage of the gate over the guarantee of $50,000. To indicate the avidity of the crowd, 9,000 fan books were sold at $1 each.

In protest against John Lennon's comment that The Beatles were more popular than Christ, the pickets outside bore hand-lettered signs with Biblical phrases. One read, "Beware False Prophets." An elderly woman wearing blue, lowcut tennis shoes was mocked by a group of teenagers, but there was no disturbance. One individual, handing out tracts, remarked, "We are protesting against the atheistic, anti-Christ Beatles. It's a sad day for America when we fall for this. It's straight out of the pits of Hell."

During the evening show, the Reverend Thomas Miller, Pastor of the Calvary Bible Presbyterian Church, arranged a concert of sacred music in the Rainier Room at the center, with baritone soloist Fague Springmann. About 250 persons attended.

Asked at a thronged press conference in the Coliseum what their reaction to this was, Lennon quipped. "Yeah, we'll be there." More than sixty persons jammed a small room in the Coliseum, which The Beatles didn't leave during their day-long stay here, and the quartet seemed blasé about the questioning.

Casually clad without neckties, The Beatles were affable for twenty minutes, often interspersing humorous asides with their answers. At the outset, Tony Barrow, the senior press agent, explicitly laid out rules for the conference and reiterated there would be no wedding here.

As photographers crowded the table, on which four microphones sat, Paul McCartney whistled, and Ringo Starr lit a cigarette. Lennon, in amber-lensed glasses, and George Harrison sat blank-faced, responding casually to appeals to smile.

In Flat Liverpool accents, The Beatles insisted that much of what they said had been exaggerated or twisted out of context. Lennon said, when queried about the almost year delay response to his remark about Christ, "Because nobody thought of what to do with it before then."

Additional criticism that their song lyrics were an affront to Christian morality elicited this response "He needs his mind straightened out," Harrison noted. And, Lennon observed, "He can't have been listening, can he?"

Whether such reactions have hurt attendance on this tour, McCartney noted, "There apparently are more people at these shows than the last. The press keeps telling you 'It's hurt you,' and our manager says 'No.' Whom do you believe? Our manager."

Offered the opportunity to discuss American foreign policy, Lennon softly demurred, "No, thank you."

It was fairly light-hearted, altogether. Harrison said of his troupe, "We can stand each other better now than when we first met." And, Lennon summed it all up by saying, "We don't intend anything. That's the trouble."

The Beatles were made honorary citizens of Washington State by Mary Ellen Shogren of Olympia, under the signature of Lud Kramer, Secretary of State. The Beatles then returned to their bare-walled dressing room, with just a few chairs and benches along the walls.

The evening crowd was slightly unrulier than the afternoon, though both were largely well-mannered. Outside, many silent youngsters milled about, seeking a chance to break through the stern line of police guards. None was successful. Inside, as The Beatles closed, several frenzied handfuls tried to rush the stage lemming-like, while flashbulbs flickered like heat lightning.

After The Beatles fled in a black limousine with a police and sheriff's escort, they boarded their plane at Sea-Tac Airport immediately, leaving about 11:30 P.M. for another appearance in Los Angeles. Inside, a monumental crush developed when several entries were sealed off to frustrate any attempt to reach the dressing rooms.

FANS REFLECT

REFLECT

■ I can remember vividly when The Beatles played here in 1966.

One memory is of riding in the backseat of our family car and passing under the sign near the Seattle Center announcing that The Beatles were going to be playing in the Coliseum. The letters were multicolored and jumbled up and down. Anyone else remember that?

Years later I worked with a woman who said that there was an underground passageway between the Center grounds and a Catholic school that used to be near the Center. She said that The Beatles used it on at least one occasion to sneak out of the Center. She also said she was a student at the school at the time.

—Anonymous

I'll never forget the shows here in Seattle in '64 and '66.

The Fab Four stayed overnight in our fair town at the Edgewater Hotel on Elliott Bay, the harbor adjacent to the city. They popularized fishing out of the window of their room, which many rock personalities have done since. Later, to capitalize on their popularity and the hysteria of the times, someone bought the carpet out of the rooms they stayed in and sold scraps for $1 each.

In '66, it was a much more sophisticated show in many ways. The sound system was better and the crowd was a bit more subdued so you were able to hear the music.

—Pete F.

I was at the '66 show and the opening act was The Cyrkle. They sang "Red Rubber Ball" and threw the ball out to the crowd. I was lucky to sit in the 12th row, front and center. I thought I was in heaven!! I could hear it all although my family outside doubted it. We were on vacation from New Jersey, and since I missed The Beatles in Philadelphia, I told my dad that I wouldn't leave Seattle until I got to see The Beatles. We didn't leave until after the concert. It was great!!

—Karen B.

Journal

plane around, returned to the hangar, and let N.D. off, along with Estelle of The Ronettes, and their road manager, Joey. It takes a lot of guts to do something like that, or a lot of fear. Next, when we finally taxied out to the takeoff position, it didn't help matters when I looked out the window and saw firetrucks following us down the runway with their blue lights flashing.

After we took off, Tom Dawes, George H. and I sat together in the back of the plane. It was late, the lights were low, and most everyone was dozing or asleep. In the dark someone passed me a cigarette with a small piece of hashish smoldering on the tip. I sucked in some of the harsh smoke and passed it on. It burned my throat. Somehow the subject of Bob Dylan came up and George remarked on the influence Dylan had on The Beatles, saying he had really blown their minds when they first heard him.

I really dug it when Bob went electric and released Like a Rolling Stone, but a lot of the folk purists hated it.

The old plane got us back to Los Angeles, but not until almost five o'clock in the morning. Another long day on The Beatles' tour.

LOS ANGELES

■ TODAY

Following an agreement reached by Chicago's civic leaders to adopt an open housing program in metropolitan areas, Dr. Martin Luther King called off his 3,000 person march into an all-white section of Chicago.

Hurricane Faith, with winds at 140 mph, veered away from the Caribbean on an erratic course for the open ocean. Weather forecasters warn that it could change course and head back toward the Bahamas.

This year the electric guitar gained prominance in rock music due partially to the popularity and virtuosity of U.S. rock musician, Jimi Hendrix.

Due to Truth in Packaging regulations, Kelloggs disclosed that Apple Jacks, which had been introduced the previous year, was 55 percent sugar.

The Baltimore Orioles defeated the Los Angeles Dodgers in the 1966 World Series.

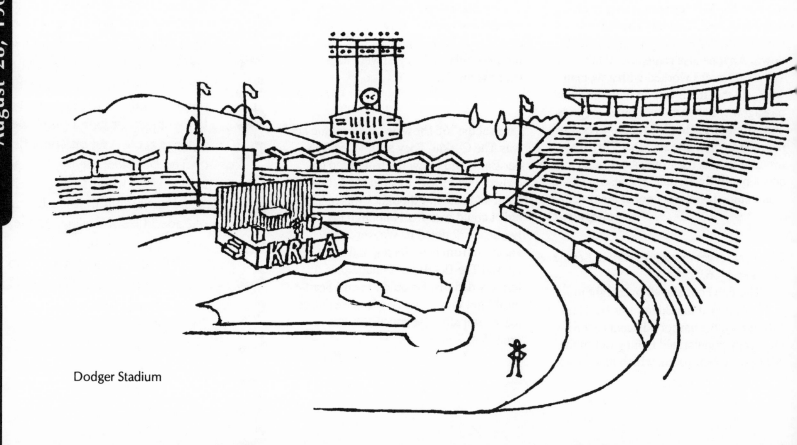

Dodger Stadium

Marty Fried, drummer for The Cyrkle, poses next to Ringo's bass drum.

Journal

Friday, August 26, 1966:

The Beatles are staying in a house on Curson Terrace, up in the Hollywood hills.

George gave me his phone number there, so I called him from my room at the Hotel Knickerbocker. He sent their limousine to pick me up and take me over there.

What a pad. Very spacious. Derek Taylor, and his wife and children, were visiting.

I wandered down the hall and found Ringo playing pool with David Crosby from The Byrds. I joined them for a short while and sunk two balls in a couple of lucky shots.

Just before dinner, Derek's young son was being a little too rough with the dog and Derek tactfully cautioned him, "Be loving and gentle, loving and gentle...."

Dinner was served. The diners were Ringo, Paul, George, John, the Derek Taylors, David Crosby, and myself. We were served by the kitchen staff— roast beef and gravy, baked potatoes, broccoli, salad, rolls, and chocolate cake.

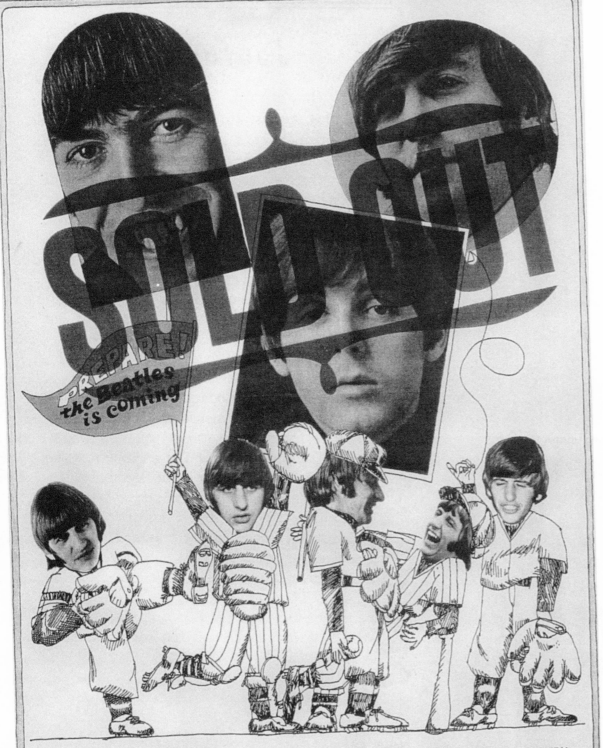

KRLA BRINGS THE BEATLES TO DODGER STADIUM, SUNDAY, AUGUST 28TH. MOVE OVER, SANDY.

The Beatles relax at the home where they stayed while in L.A.

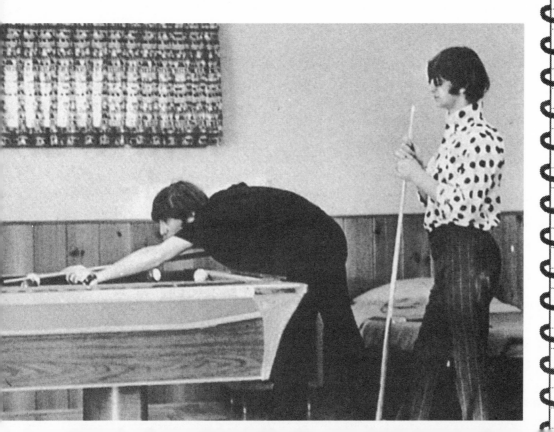

Journal

After dinner, George and I hopped into David Crosby's silver Porsche and headed down the hill into the Hollywood night. First stop was a visit with photographer Barry Feinstein and his wife, Mary Travers, of Peter, Paul & Mary. We were talking out on the balcony, which had a fantastic view of Los Angeles by night. The lights were really beautiful. It was a brief visit.

Next stop was Jim McGuinn's house. He was really nice and showed us a movie that he'd made with flashes of many colors and abstracts of many shapes. The sound track was The Beatles' Tomorrow Never Knows. It worked very well and George really enjoyed it.

Then we drove over to Cass Elliot's house. I met Peter Tork of The Monkees there and had a good chat with him. A nice guy. Denny from the Mamas & Papas and Jim McGuinn were there, as well. Had a cup of tea. There was an excited mood in the air. Some of those present were meeting George for the first time. Others knew him already. I felt like George's old friend, having traveled with The Beatles for over two weeks.

ON TOUR

with

THE BEATLES

by Judith Sims,
Editor, TeenSet Magazine

■ The only incident occurred early in The Beatles' act when several people (mostly boys) came over the back wall and ran broken-field style for the stage. The guards discouraged that in a hurry, but there was such an uproar from the crowd that The Beatles kept looking back with a "What's happening?" expression.

Once again the press party had to leave early, so we missed all the excitement of the escape. A tent in back of the stage concealed a car. Apparently, the car couldn't get out of the stadium because the exit was blocked by other vehicles. It reversed right back into the stadium, where they transferred to an armored car, but that couldn't make it through the crowd, either, so The Beatles went back to their dressing room, changed, and sat around for about two hours before they finally made it out in the limousine. (Some enterprising fans had reportedly let the air out of the armored car's tires.)

While vacationing in L.A., The Beatles went out only twice (not all four, just one or two at a time). They visited Mama Cass Elliot one night; on another occasion, Paul McCartney dropped by to see Derek Taylor, and soon George Harrison arrived with David Crosby; later Carl and Brian Wilson of the Beach Boys joined the gathering. A "pop summit," it was called.

A technician checks Ringo's equipment before the show at Dodger Stadium.

Barry and Vern perform for an enthusiastic L.A. crowd.

The Remains make a mad dash for the stage while Bob Eubanks holds the tent flap.

Journal

Later, we went on to Derek Taylor's house where John and Paul had already assembled.

Brian and Carl Wilson from the Beach Boys were there. At one point, Derek put on a Byrds record, which rubbed Crosby the wrong way. "Don't play that," he said, removing the record from the turntable.

It was interesting group of people to observe— Rock Royalty.

The Beach Boys and The Beatles!

It was funny— they were very friendly and genial, but really shy with each other.

The Beach Boys looked so clean-cut in their button-down madras shirts and khakis.

I sat quietly and sipped my orange juice.

I don't know how John got home, but I squeezed into the Porsche with George, Paul and David. It wasn't a long drive up the hill to The Beatle residence. Crosby drove me back to the Hotel Knickerbocker.

What a night!

Journal

Sunday, August 28, 1966:
We took the bus to Dodger Stadium and faced the WALL again: fifty thousand people. I couldn't *feel* any of them. The stage was in its usual distant position on second base, over a hundred feet from the audience. I felt so isolated out there trying to compete with Beatlemania. If I've learned anything from this tour, it's how insignificant I am in this whole scenario. The Beatles gave a great show and the crowd was absolutely wild!

As I was walking back to the dressing room after our set, I saw Edward G. Robinson sitting just behind the dugout. On the way home we stopped at the Hollywood Ranch Market for some snacks then went back to the Hotel Knickerbocker to sleep.

We've been talking very seriously about moving to the West Coast and beginning a new way of life. We've met some nice folks here, but we've got some talking to do when we get back to New York and Cambridge. I definitely want to spend a few days in Cambridge just to see how it feels to me now. What an INCREDIBLE tour this has been.

Adult Takes in a 'Concert'

by Jack Smith

A man who has never gone to a Beatles' concert has never really made contact with the teenage generation.

I had only one ticket Sunday night so I went to Dodger Stadium alone. A middle-aged single on the aisle.

I sat in a sea of teenagers. Two girls in the seats in front of me turned around and smiled maternally. Girls always smile maternally at older men.

I was hardly in my seat when there was a fantastic sound, like the shrieking of a sky full of jets.

"For your informaiton," said the scoreboard, "The Beatles have arrived..."

This had set off the ear-splitting din.

"And..." The shrill sound lowered—40,000 voices poised, "...are in their dressing room!"

Pandemonium.

While The Beatles were in their dressing room, we were entertained, the scoreboard said by a group called The Remains. They did look a bit left over.

While The Remains were stomping about and yelling into the microphones, the scoreboard lit up with a new message:

"Welcome all adults we converted to Beatle fans. Where are you?"

All heads within twenty feet turned my way. The two girls in front of me fawned maternally.

"Go on," said the girl on my right. "Stand up!"

I cowered in my seat. I took a deep gulp of my root beer and started coughing.

"What's the matter?" the girl asked. "You embarrassed?"

"No," I told her. "I've just got a touch of consumptive conspicuousness."

Caught With Notes

After The Remains, they gave us a group called The Cyrkle. The odd spelling came up on the scoreboard. I took out my notebook to write it down. One of the girls in front caught me at it.

"Are you a reporter?" she asked.

"Oh, no," I said, fumbling for some reasonable way out. "I'm interested in music. I'm a composer."

"Oh! What did you compose?"

"Well," I said. "Have you ever heard of 'End of a Perfect Day?'"

She shook her head.

"How about 'Nearer My God to Thee'?"

"You're kidding," she said. She looked at me with reproach.

I turned to the girl on the right. After all, she had spoken first. "Do you like the Kyrkles?" I asked.

"Kyrkles?" she shrieked. "They are CIRcles. They just spell it that way."

How skware can you get?

Fortunately, The Beatles finally came on and further conversation was impossible. They sounded just like their records, only louder.

FANS REFLECT

REFLECT

■ My girlfriend's father was a producer for Angel Records, Capitol's classical label. Capitol gave him four tickets, two on the field level. The field seats were great, ten rows up from the field. When we sat down and saw that the stage was set up on second base, our hearts sank. It looked miles away. My girlfriend and I were intellectual Beatle fans, meaning we NEVER screamed; we really wanted to hear the music!

We observed Edward G. Robinson sitting two rows in front of us. We didn't realize he was so cool. A few minutes before The Beatles came on, the crowd was in a frenzy. Suddenly, Eddy G. stood up and walked out, and never returned! I noticed he had cotton in his ears.

In the car we saw an ambulance leaving Dodger Stadium. Later, we heard that's how The Beatles left the Stadium.

—*Linda*

My ticket cost $6! I was seated right behind the third base dugout . . . pretty good seats for a ballpark. I do remember The Remains, Bobby Hebb and The Ronettes. Didn't The Cyrkle also play that night?

I remember being jolted from head to toe when The Beatles were introduced and emerged from the dugout just below me. The electricity was amazing. The feeling when they emerged from the dugout was nothing like I'd ever felt— just noise and excitement! I turned to look over

at my very cool older cousin, and the hair on the back of his neck was standing up! He turned to look at me with a look of excitement and absolute wide-eyed amazement!

I was amazed at how well I could hear The Beatles over the din. Remember that bass lick at the end of "Paperback Writer" where McCartney trills that note? I could feel the power of his amp vibrating my seat. Fantastic!

The Beatles bolted off stage and ran into a tent that had been constructed just stage left, and then emerged a limo that maneuvered through the third base bullpen. The kids, however, were waiting, and about 100 kids dropped from the stands onto the top of the limo. Jeez.

—*Gary Packer*

I saw The Beatles in Los Angeles in 1966. My wife saw them in Chicago the same year.

Years later we both worked on McCartney's recording projects and I met George Martin.

I got to ask Paul about the '66 Los Angeles concert and he told me that they (The Beatles) were just as thrilled to play as we were to watch!

—*Dave*

I was at the Chavez Ravine (Dodger Stadium) show in Los Angeles and remember The Remains set pretty clearly, since it was the only decent rock and roll on the bill apart from the headliners.

I also remember a great line in the *Los Angeles Times* after the concert. They sent their regular "grownup" columnist, Jack Smith, to cover the show from an adult's perspective, and in his droll way, he said something like "the next group was called The Remains. They *did* look a little left-over."

—*Richard*

I was a teenager, and I went with my buddy, Chris Reed, whose real name is Bob Issacson, but we called him Chris Reed at the time. We had on-lawn passes which we got from Carl Wilson of The Beach Boys, and Earl Leaf, who was a photographer at the time. Neil Aspinall had to sign them. We were on the lawn by the stage.

When the show was over, we went downstairs in the dugout. We got to meet and talk with The Beatles. When they tried to leave Dodger Stadium the first time, they couldn't get out. They had to drive the limousine around by the gate and couldn't get out. So, they had to come back and wait awhile, and then try again.

Finally, everyone cleared out and The Beatles left and went to a gas station in an armored car. They switched to a limousine at the gas station in Silver Lake on Sunset. But, before they did that The Beatles stopped at a liquor store to pick up a few things like coke and chewing gum. Then, we pulled into that same liquor store to get some Diet Rite and there was this dog in the store that started to growl at us. We took our Beatle on-lawn passes and flashed them to the dog. The dog quit growling.

I remember going to a party afterwards up on Curson to a big house, up on the hill above Hollywood Boulevard. I remember I went with Jim McGuinn of The Byrds. He gave me a ride up to the house. He had a red Porsche. We went in and all of The Beatles were there.

—*Rodney Bingenheimer*

■ TODAY

Nurses in San Francisco walked out of their jobs to strike for higher wages. Many patients had to be transferred to hospitals outside the area to receive treatment.

With 705,000 South Vietnamese troops under arms, there have been 67,000 desertions this year. For the first time, the Vietnamese government has taken stern steps to send soldiers before a firing squad if they are caught.

This year the Freedom of Information Act was passed by Congress.

The Black Panther Party was formed by Huey Newton and Bobby Seale. It was a militant Black political organization which advocated the use of violence in obtaining Black rights.

Record label EMI Records Ltd. of England used the monies received from the sale of Beatle records to begin development on the computed axial tomography (CAT) scanner, which would revolutionize modern medicine.

Robert Sanderson Mullikan won the 1966 Nobel Prize for his research on atoms and their molecular bonds.

Golden Gate Bridge—San Francisco.

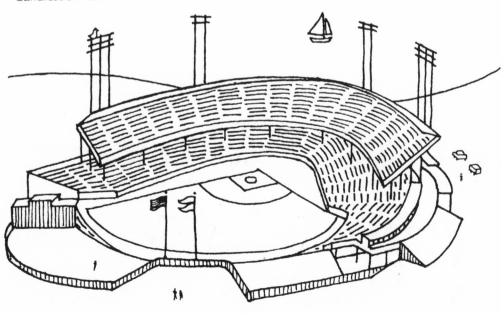

Candlestick Park

Journal

Monday, August 29th, 1966

Awoke at noon, showered, and met the bus to the plane. We're going to San Francisco for the last concert, but we'll fly back tonight, our last flight with The Beatles. I'm sitting in the private jet, complete with TV, stereo headphones, two stereo outputs, and horrible Muzak.

Tonight was the last concert of the tour at Candlestick Park. We had a little trouble getting into the park, due to a locked gate. The bus driver took the bus out to the far perimeter of the parking lot in an effort to avoid fans. The fans eventually headed for our bus, so we started moving again with the fans in hot pursuit. The bus finally got into the park, after driving around the neighborhood for awhile.

On stage, a wild sea wind was blowing in every direction. There was a double fence around the stage. The only entrance was behind the drums. The audience was about 200 feet away—much farther than usual. It made us feel _extremely_ isolated from the audience. But it was the last show, and we were determined to have a good time. All the acts did a great job to wind up the tour on a high note. The nineteenth and final show is complete now, and we all feel as good, if not better, than we did at the start of the tour!

ON TOUR

with

THE **BEATLES**

by Judith Sims,
Editor, TeenSet Magazine

On the bus enroute to Candlestick Park.

■ The next day, Monday, was the last concert date of the tour. We gathered at the hotel for the limo ride to the airport—jet this time, which meant a short flight. We were already beginning to get that "It's almost over" bluesy feeling.

In San Francisco, we transferred to a bus which drove us to Candlestick Park. This provided some light entertainment when we arrived at the park. It seems that the gate through which we were supposed to enter wasn't open when the bus arrived, so the bus went around in circles—literally, in circles—all around the parking lot, trailing cars with fans hanging out the windows and also trailing girls who could enter the Olympics as track stars. We then left the

park, drove around a few hills, turned around, came back, took a few turns around the parking lot again and then, finally, through a gate (and through several hundred fans) into the stadium.

Before the performance, we had our last goodbye taping session in The Beatles' dressing room. They had just finished eating, so amidst coffee cups and tape recorders, we all took our leave, so to speak.

George was in the process of drawing a weird purple face among green leaves, and Paul had just finished a yellow and orange impressionistic drawing, which he gave to Kenny Edwards. The atmosphere was getting a little heavy with end-of-the-tour nostalgia.

San Francisco had a past history of wild crowds, and this time the security guards and The Beatles' security people weren't taking any chances. We were told to leave the stage area extra early and wait in the bus just in case we had to make a quick getaway, or in case The Beatles might have to transfer to the bus for their escape. There were 25,000 screaming fans at Candlestick, but no riots. But, we didn't know there wouldn't be a riot, so we dutifully trundled off to the bus halfway through the show and waited. And waited. And waited. We were sure The Beatles were already back in L.A. before the bus revved up and moved out.

It wasn't an easy exit—the fans were still there, and they didn't give up easily. Apparently, the armored car had been sufficient to rescue The Beatles.

On the plane heading for L.A., The Beatles faced another hazard of their particular profession—lack of privacy. They were forced to change from their stage suits to regular clothes in front of just about everyone, but they handled it discreetly. They're past masters at handling lack of privacy with aplomb.

Since I hadn't had time to speak with Paul in San Francisco, he sat down next to me on the plane, and we talked all the way back to L.A. We discussed the possibility and probability of a 1967 tour, and he talked at great length about tentative plans. All four Beatles want to cut down on their performing time so they can concentrate more on recording, which they feel is their best way of expressing their creativity. "We're not very good performers, actually," he said. "We're better in a recording studio where we can control things and work on it until it's right. With performing there's so much that can go wrong, and you can't go back over it and do it right."

The flight back was far too short, and when we touched down in L.A., it was time for the real, final goodbye. Three weeks of Beatles had become a sort of delightful

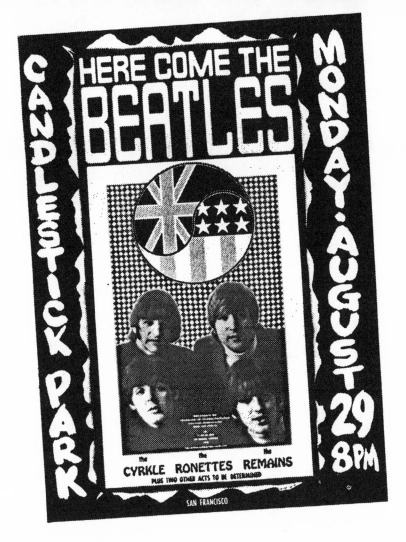

We're on the 707-Boeing Super Deluxe—television, candlelight, stereo, steak dinner, and red wine. Superb feeling! We should be back in L.A. within an hour or so.

When we landed, I asked for The Beatles' autographs (I saved this for the last minute). George wrote his address in my address book, and we had a portrait photo taken on the plane, sitting together— hope it comes out. It was time to say goodbye to The Beatles. John said, "Whenever you're within a hundred miles, look us up." We shook hands, and I bid them each "Cheerio."
Back to the Knickerbocker Hotel to bed.

ADDRESSES
WENDY HANSON
MAY.FAIR. 5248

GEORGE. H.
-"KINFAUNS"
CLAREMONT.
DRIVE
ESHER —
SURREY
ENGLAND.

habit, and none of us could imagine life without them around.

We all said goodbye again and pretended to be cheerful about "see you again soon" and all that. But, it wouldn't be soon at all—it would be at least another year before our lives would be brightened and enlightened by four young Liverpudlians.

Most of the press party gathered in the hotel bar after that. The men were trying to look casual, but it wasn't working. We all sat around and looked abandoned and bereft. We had, for a brief mourning period, lost our identity and that wonderful sense of belonging. All would be "back to normal" in a few days we assured ourselves.

That was the problem. After being with The Beatles, who wanted to go back to normal? Our yellow submarine had surfaced, and the crew had dispersed.

■ SAN FRANCISCO EXAMINER ■

Beatles Strike Out at Ball Park

by Philip Elwood

Precisely thirty minutes and eleven tunes after they mounted their caged performance tower over second base at Candlestick Park last night, The Beatles cascaded downward into a revved up armored truck, and vanished behind a cloud of right field dust into the night.

Some 25,000 spectators, exhilarated and excited, were left much like a jammed ballpark crowd that had just seen the winning homerun ball disappear into the bleachers—numbed by the sudden end of the spectacle, and disappointed by the brevity of the climactic event.

Master of ceremonies, Gene Nelson, had earlier joked, "With the breezes out here, you will see The Beatles, but they may hear them better in Alameda." A funny line (one of many by Nelson and Johnny Holiday), but inaccurate; everyone could hear most of The Beatles' songs, if at times drowned by screams. But, none of the paying customers could see clearly or feel any personal involvement with the four young Englishmen in the distance.

The concert, as such, must be termed a bust. Sure, Paul McCartney's remarkably pure tone on "Yesterday" was good to hear; "I Wanna Be Your Man," "Day Tripper," "Paperback Writer" and the others came out just like on the records. But, concerts, even by The Beatles, should mean more than four little figures far away creating wind-distorted sounds inferior in quality to the totally familiar studio recorded versions.

Ringo's drums, such as they are, were inaudible, and we didn't even get his hilarious vocal on "Yellow Submarine." It wasn't included. As a matter of fact, nothing from the new, delightful album was on the show, probably because special sound effects and backgrounds are impossible in ballpark appearances.

For thousands of expectant youngsters, once the thrill of The Beatles actually running out of the dugout and onto the stand had worn off, the principal diversion came in cheering the beginning of each two minute tune and then watching the boys who broke through the centerfield fence as they played tag with the police.

It was, of course, a fascinating evening from a spectator's point of view—observing the colorful crowd, not the stage.

The whole evening's production was an expensive and thoroughly synchronized bit of highly commercial machinery. Each of the preliminary throw-away acts did their stint to indifferent crowd response, and soaked up the minutes until The Beatles appeared. Then came the screams, the thousands of flash-bulbs (God knows what those little cameras captured from 100 yards away) . . . and for a half-hour, it happened.

1966, Hello

Janet Jackson
Stacy Lattisaw

1966, Goodbye

Lenny Bruce
Montgomery Clift
Walt Disney
William Frawley
Bobby Fuller
(Bobby Fuller Four)
Hedda Hopper
Buster Keaton
S.S. Kresge
Chester Nimitz
Sophie Tucker
Clifton Webb
Ed Wynn

Eighteen days and fourteen cities later, The Beatles play their last concert ever on August 29, 1966, at Candlestick Park in San Francisco, California.

FANS REFLECT

REFLECT

■ I wasn't exactly rattling jewelry, but I paid my $7.50. The cheaper seats went for one and two dollars less. While those in my section heard The Beatles' performance quite well, many people left Candlestick Park complaining that they couldn't hear.

I filmed the complete day's activities, from the building of the stage through The Beatles' final bows. And, I did it right out in the open. Like everyone else, I hadn't a clue that this was the last concert, or that what my fifteen-year-old hands were shooting would become the only complete chronicle of the day's events.

Security-wise, the show was uneventful, including the mere two handfuls of boys who jumped the outfield fence. They didn't get far and fell quick prey for some of the 200+ rent-a-cops. Those of us in the stands were orderly. That's what I remember, and that's what my film shows. We were warned that to even be on the field would mean certain expulsion and possible arrest! Only those who avoided the price of admission jumped over the fence. These were the "bad boys"—some of the incorrigible locals from the ghetto neighborhood surrounding Candlestick.

For extra security, the San Francisco stage was protected by a double row of fencing. Marty Fried of The Cyrkle is one of the few who had a stage-level view.

An armored car waited, engine running, beside the stage throughout the show. This was their ultimate escape hatch, should all hell break loose and the fans rush onto the field. It's a wonder anyone could play music in such a paranoid environment. There comes a point when they can't. The Beatles were clearly nearing that point. They gave no impression of it during the show. But, the extraordinary security precautions gave them away.

Was this to be the last concert? Paul McCartney had asked Tony Barrow to tape record the show. Both Lennon and McCartney were snapping photos during their walk to the stage. Harrison can be clearly seen doing the same in my color footage.

—*Barry Hood*

Barry Hood, whose film of the Candlestick Park concert is called, ONE LAST TIME, can be contacted at 1-800-2-Videos; from outside the U.S., 541-895-5007; or P.O. Box 413, Creswell, OR 97326.

Believe it or not, I attended the Candlestick Park concert in August of '66 with a girlfriend. I was more interested in her than the music, which suffered from poor sound amplification.

—*Anonymous*

Yeah, I was there too. Stadium public address systems were not made to handle concert music. Couldn't hear much over the screaming. And, the stage on second base looked so far away.

—*Jeff*

Photo of Ringo taken from the only entrance to the stage.

Drummer N.D. Smart and keyboardist Bill Briggs of The Remains.

Journal

Tuesday, August 30th, 1966
Los Angeles:

We had interviews scheduled all day with KRLA Radio's *Beat* Magazine, and *Teen Screen* Magazine.

I'm feeling kind of low today— having been on The Beatles' tour was much too exciting. But, one thing is true, I feel lucky to have spent some time WITH The Beatles. They're so bright, funny, and enlightened. After three weeks on The Beatles' tour, normal life looks pretty dull. I didn't expect to feel such a let-down after leaving The Beatles' party. Now, it's back to the mundane reality of being in The Remains.

To bed early; 10:30 P.M.

Wednesday, August 31st, 1966:

Did an interview today with KFWB. "Channel 98-Color Radio." Tonight, I am back in the hotel room again, #717. Vern is leaving for Boston tomorrow morning and Ed is going to San Francisco to visit Peter Childs. Briggs and I will stay on until we feel like going to San Francisco— then back to New York City.

The clock just struck midnight— it's now September 1st.

Goodnight.

The Beatle Tour

by Rochelle Reed

■ "Playing the Beatle tour was like performing in a closet with the lights off," confessed Briggs, one of The Remains who wandered up to *The BEAT* office the day after their last performance.

"It was a matter of an instrument being on or off," chimed in their road manager, "with no room for subtleties. Either the crowds could hear or they couldn't."

Apparently, U.S. crowds could hear the group, because The Remains admitted reaction "was better than we'd thought it would be."

The BEAT was surprised to see The Remains at all, considering that they had just concluded twenty-four performances that at best could be described as "hectic."

Actually, we didn't see *all* The Remains. Briggs, Barry and Vern showed up but N.D., their drummer, was somewhere between Hollywood and San Francisco.

"He didn't make it back," said Barry. "He got on the plane in San Francisco, and then got off and said he just couldn't do it."

Flying Phobia

N.D. has a phobia about flying, and left the plane once before when the craft threw sparks over Seattle. But, N.D. used to be an acrobat and walk tightropes 300 feet off the ground. "Oh well," said Briggs, "That's N.D."

The three Remains, although tired, were almost radiating with new ideas for their act. "It's like closing a chapter in our careers," Barry said. "We're thinking about different directions we can take musically," Vern added. "Maybe we won't even play for a while, just for a kick," chimed in Briggs. "We need time to think the whole thing out."

Vern admitted that the tour has made the group "hungrier for fame" than ever before. "It opened our eyes where they had been closed before," added Barry, and Briggs continued, "We learned that what's honest, both musically and personally, is best."

How did The Remains get on the tour in the first place? "A few people up there like us a lot," according to Briggs.

The Remains, who are noted for the true hard rock that they play, opened all The Beatle shows, and then backed up Bobby Hebb and The Ronettes.

Never Back

"Backing was something we told ourselves we'd never do," Barry said. They almost refused the tour before deciding maybe the excitement and fame was worth it all.

"We only had an hour and a half

'Like Playing in a Closet'

to practice with the other groups before we had to back them in our first show," Barry said. So, they decided not to even try to simulate the backup sound that Bobby and The Ronettes use on their records.

Rather then sound like a poor imitation, Briggs explained, "We played our way, and Bobby and The Ronettes liked it. At San Francisco, it turned into a way-out jazz session in the middle of 'Sunny'."

The largest welcome for the tour, the group decided after much debate, was in Chicago, whereas Detroit held the distinction of having the most junk thrown onstage. Memphis was infamous, the group said, because someone threw a cherry bomb at the platform.

But, The Remains came through without any major hang-ups, and are now eagerly looking to the future and the "embellishments" they will make on their sound.

The group has a new album com-ing out, which they consider the best of what they used to do. It's called The Remains.

"Major diversity" is planned for their sound. Once known only as a hard rock blues band, they will now go softer and do the songs that they've always wanted to include in their repertoire.

"Right now, our audience is growing up," says Briggs, "and also calming down. They will appreciate talent even more than before."

So The Remains plan a search into who they really are—musically and personally. They credit The Beatles for giving them "a better insight in our search."

"They were everything I'd hoped they'd be," Barry said.

Barry became good friends with George Harrison, and the two spent many hours listening to sitar music that George brought over on tape. In Los Angeles, the two slipped out one night and visited some of the pop groups who call L.A. their home.

"It was great, really finding where these people are," Barry said.

Though New England, mainly Boston, is home for The Remains, they hope to become more popular in other parts of the country. Until now, they have concentrated on college tours and large clubs in the East.

Barry Tashian, lead guitar player, has often been called "the white James Brown." William Briggs, or just Briggs as he is known, is a tall, sandy blond organist with the group. A talkative, bright-eyed musician, he would like to live in Balboa for awhile "without any shoes and not play at all, just for kicks."

"Crazy Things"

Vern Miller, the smallest of The Remains, was once a classical musician, and plays just about everything, including guitar. He wants to branch out into electronic music. N.D. Smart is the drummer for the group and, as yet, unmet by *The BEAT* staff. "He used to want to jump off bridges in Boston," the group explained. "And he does crazy, incredible things."

N.D. is the most recent member of the group, and used to play for Paul, of Peter, Paul and Mary, when he recorded alone.

The Remains now stand where many groups would like to—they have received the widest exposure any group could possibly hope for and "learned a lot." Though they are "hungrier for fame," they are also humbled a little. They are eager to attack their music and remake it to fit what they have become. Then, with minor embellishments and major diversity, they will put it to work.

THE MUSIC STILL REMAINS

When I look back at The Beatles last tour, I'm amazed at what an impact it had on my life. In the weeks following the tour, I became very discourage, realizing that The Remains would never be as great as The Beatles. That September, Epic Records released our first album, The Remains. By that time I had disbanded The Remains and, consequently, we did not tour the album at all.

There was a change in the air. Rock 'n roll as we knew it was a thing of the past. The only alternative I could find was to expand my musical boundaries to include both country music and rhythm and blues. I moved to California and played with Gram Parsons in the original Flying Burrito Brothers. There was a flourishing musical community in L.A. with Leon Russell, Neil Young, Jesse Ed Davis, J.J. Cale, Chris Hillman and many others. We immersed ourselves in all types of music from George Jones, Hank Williams, and Buck Owens, to B.B. King, Otis Redding, and Lowell Fulson. It was a time to recover and rejuvinate myself after the impact of The Beatles tour.

After several years of experimenting with different musical forms, I began to focus on country music. Gram Parsons invited me to record with him on his first album for Warner Brothers. There I met the lovely Emmylou Harris, my harmony partner on Gram's album.

From my experience with Gram, I formed my own band with my wife, Holly, and played country music throughout the 1970s.

In 1980, Emmylou Harris invited me to join the Hot Band. I spent ten years in her band, recording and touring worldwide. It was fantastic experience.

Now, thirty years after The Beatles tour, I'm still playing music for a living. Holly and I have rcorded a number of albums, traveled around the world and managed to raise a family.

Recently, we watched The Beatles Anthology and were reminded of the tremendous influence they had on all of us. Their songs are now solid classics. Looking back, I now know that touring with The Beatles was one of the most exciting experiences I've ever had, and I feel extremely fortunate to have had the opportunity to meet them and work with them.

Bill Briggs
Keyboardist, vocals
The Remains

■ I remember being very nervous in Chicago before we went on for our first show. I was in a panic because we couldn't use our own amps. Terry or Bill Hanley sat at the side of the stage with a huge amp with tall blue glowing tubes—very science fiction-like.

I remember twenty-eight states in thirty days. The Beatles seemed very bored. I have this image of dirty clothes and sweaty band uniforms. In each city, Ed Freeman always had to find dry cleaners. I can still see the red clay at the baseball parks and the fans straining at chain link fences.

Sometimes it was hard to get food before shows. Sometimes I felt trapped in the hotels. Once, in Seattle, I hid under the bed (I was depressed and hungry).

I remember smoking pot with George on the tarmac outside the plane. A big circle would form and someone would take out pre-rolled African pot with a cardboard filter inserted in the end. *Good shit.*

It's just like present day—the easiet part is actually playing the music. It's the getting there, setting up, personal hassles, equipment hassles, and sound hassles that are difficult. the last thing on your mind is actually playing the music. I have a recurring dream that I spend all my time setting up and solving problems, and never actually get to play. Wonder what that means?

I remember Ed Freeman tuning the electric 12-string guitar onstage and playing Elizabethen "lute" music. Sounded great.

N.D. Smart
Drummer
The Remains

■ I remember when we introduced ourselves to The Beatles on the plane. That was the first time we met them. They were sitting in the back of the plane. We walked back there and we just happened to see them and our eyes met. We each took turns introducing ourselves—and Barry introduced Billy Briggs to John Lennon and George Harrison, who were sitting together. Barry said ". . . and this is Bill Briggs" and John Lennon looked at Bill Briggs and said, "Briggs and Mortar!" He was into puns as a kind of a personal habit—á la *A Spaniard in the Works.*

Paul McCartney was the most unapproachable of all The Beatles, in my mind. I'll never forget one time I saw him get off the plane and approach a group of fans just so he could refuse to sign autographs. He walked over to them and walked near them and just taunted them. That actually happened.

When we were leaving Memphis, we were on the bus with all the members of the tour, waiting for The Beatles and the plane. As we were talking, everybody started singing each others' hit records; Bobby Hebb had "Sunny" out, so we were all singing "Sunny." We sang a Ronettes' song and when we got to The Cyrkle we sang "Red Rubber Ball." When we got to us, everybody was a little embarrased. They didn't know any of our songs, because we didn't have a hit. By this time we were on the airport runway, and the plane was just arriving. We were still waiting for The Beatles. Nobody wanted to get on the plane, so we started to sing "Yellow Submarine," and The Beatles pulled up. As we were singing, John Lennon walked over and started singing along with us, clapping his hands and directing us all through the song. It meant a lot to everybody.

One time I got the courage to sit down with John Lennon and we were small talking when a DJ from St. Louis sat down opposite us. He was on the tour for just a couple legs. He was going to be drafted into the service. So, the moral issue of going to war came up. The Vietnam War was raging at that time. We started discussing whether he should be a conscientious objector or not. I was really touched by the fact that John, Lennon really gave this guy a lot of personal attention.

John really had compassion for what this guy was going through. This guy was touched by the fact that John Lennon was taking a personal interest in him. John said that no one could make you go to war if you really didn't want to. The guy was struggling with the issue because he was raised traditionally. John was compassionate about the fact that he was struggling with the issue.

One of my most vivid recollections of the tour was sitting with John on the plane, sharing a joint, something we would do ocassionally. I was seventeen years old and this was the most exciting thing that ever happened to me, but it also turned out to be one of the most sobering and depressing as well. Before, I had thought of myself as an individual—an original kind of person. But, the fact was, that I had Beatle shoes on; I had John Lennon glasses on; and I had a John Lennon haircut. When I looked at him, I suddenly realized that I was just a cheap imitation of the real thing—confronting the real McCoy. Instead of enjoying the rest of the tour, I realized that I had to go on a journey to find out who I was.

I had a fear of flying, and had a premonition about it. All I could think was that I was going to be one of the unknown people who got killed with The Beatles. One time, I actually got off the plane and took a commercial flight to the next job, rather than go on the charter. One of The Ronettes and I got off that plane and went to the next gig together, because I had this premonition that I was going to be killed with The Beatles. Of course, it didn't happen; I stopped the plane. The plane was on the runway ready to take off, and I made them *turn* around and take me back. That was reported in *16 Magazine.*

When we went to play in Cincinnati, it rained and the concert had to be postponed until the next day. I got to spend some time in my hometown. Cincinnati is right next to Dayton, where I was sort of a local star. I spent some time with The Beatles before the show with my girlfriend. I got to introduce my girlfriend to The Beatles.

While we were with The Beatles, the promoter came up to The Beatles and gave them a paper bag. In that paper bag was thousands of dollars in cash that The Beatles got paid under the table for that particular gig.

I went with Mal Evans, The Beatles' road manager, when The Beatles went to meet Elvis in Memphis. It was a very poignant, weird moment. Nobody, of course, cared about me; so, I just watched this thing go down. Elvis and The Beatles really couldn't relate to each other. They had almost nothing to say to each other. It was like two fast guns in town. I watched how they eyeballed each other. It was cordial and everything, but, the Elvis entourage was kind of defensive about The Beatles being there.

On the ride over, I talked to Mal about The Beatles. I kind of got my feelings hurt, because I wasn't getting a lot of attention from them during the tour. I told Mal that I thought they were stuck up. Mal said I was misjudging them, that they were just so busy they didn't have time to get to know everybody. Evans said, "Hey, why don't you come up and see the guys. They can't go out and sometimes they just want companionship."

I was talking to Harrison and Lennon one day and I said, "You know, I feel sorry for you guys, not being able to go out or anything." And, George Harrison sat me down and said, "Look—we put ourselves in this position on purpose. We planned to be big. We plotted to be big, and this is what we got. Don't feel sorry for us. We're getting what we wanted."

On the way into Memphis, they thought something violent was going to happen. Driving into Memphis from the airport, we had to lie down, because they thought snipers might shoot us.

The Cyrkle

Vern Miller
Bass, vocals
The Remains

■ I remember...

John Kurland making a deal with Brian Epstein. The Beatles could use our P.A. system if we could use their amps for the entire tour.

Surrounded by police from Memphis to Coliseum.

Mal Evans' "Sin Kit"—a violin case with whiskey bottle and cigarettes.

I blew up Paul's Super Beatle Amp at Suffolk Downs in Boston. Thank God for the Vox Representative.

At Shea, our limo broke down and I remember girls screaming and rocking it.

Someone came up to The Beatles' suite with some hookers. George said, "No thanks, it's just a 'huka.'" George seemed like the Beatle with a lot of internal strength and spiritual depth.

The Beatles were pale and short. Ringo was the funniest, most down-to-earth. When we came out of George's room one night after listening to Ravi Shankar tapes, Ringo was in the living room sitting cross-legged on the floor with his eyes glued to TV. The station had gone off, but he was mesmerized by the test pattern.

Ed Freeman
Road Manager for
    The Remains
Official photographer for
    The Beatles' tour.

■ Looking back, what strikes me most is what an earth-shaking event that tour appeared to be at the time, and yet how modest a production it was by current day rock tour standards. As a roadie/road manager, I do have a rather warped perspective, but what I remember is that there were five bands on the tour, and *all* the equipment for all five bands, including The Beatles—drums, guitars, keyboards, amps, everything—fit in one stretch van. And, there was a grand total of three roadies—Mal (Malcom) Evans, Mike Owens and myself, to handle all of it. Now they have three roadies for one band's drum kit.

I'm the only surviving roadie from that tour. Mike was killed in a traffic accident a year or two after the tour, and Mal Evans died, I believe, a few years later.

There was also a guy from Vox who came along just to fix The Beatles' guitar amps in case they blew up, which they did on a regular basis. They were Super Beatle amps—very new at the time, and very temperamental.

By modern day standards, the sound was pathetic. Only a few of the gigs—New York, Boston, and a few other places, had any dedicated P.A., whatever that was, and the result was often unintelligible noise. Not that most people cared a lot, they were too busy screaming to hear anything. But, we had a riot in Cleveland when three thousand people rushed the stage because they couldn't hear. I don't blame them.

In St. Louis, we played a baseball stadium. The instrument sound came off the stage, which was set up on second base. The vocals came out of the house P.A., which consisted of one speaker in back of the bleachers behind home plate. The vocals were at least a second late by the time they reached the stage, making it virtually impossible for the guys on stage to hear what they were doing.

It was raining on and off, and the concert promoter hadn't put an awning over the stage. It would have cost him an extra two hundred bucks—so everybody was getting soaked. Not a good idea with electric guitars and microphones. Mal gave me a big outlet box with a big AC cord plugged into it and told me to pull it whenever the first person on stage collapsed from any electric shock. I sat there the whole concert, soaking wet, my feet on the box and my hands on the cord. There were sparks flying all over the place. I remember that every time Paul bumped into the mic, which was almost every beat, there were sparks going between him and the mic, but nobody died and the concert went on, mostly to an empty house by the end of it because it was really pouring by then.

There wasn't a whole lot of time to set up the equipment for each gig. Now, it takes three days and a crew of fifty to set up a stadium concert; but for us, it was more like three people and one hour. One time we left Boston in the morning, played a four and an eight o'clock show in Memphis, and slept in Cincinnati that same night. The show in Memphis was delayed because of a bomb scare. Just before the tour started, John had

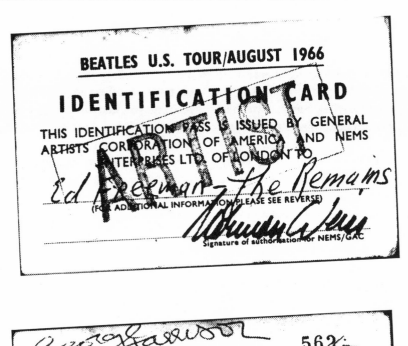

into an ashtray. We ran around after him, picking up his discarded roaches as fast as he dropped them. They were the size of Pall Malls.

Barry and I sat in a room with George, and the two played guitar together. Every once in a while, Mal Evans would come in and pull George out of the room. George would come back in a couple of minutes, saying something like, "Oh, she was pretty all right, but not for me." They would then resume playing. Mal was scouring the groupies in the hotel lobby — there were hundreds of them — and escorting a few choice picks up to the suite.

There was a fad at the time among teenage girls of making long, zigzag chains out of chewing gum wrappers and giving them to boys as an expression of affection. After every concert, the stage would be littered with chains. Sometimes, girls would come up to the stage as we were cleaning up, with incredibly long chains — forty, fifty feet — and tearfully beg us to give them to their favorite Beatle. All sorts of favors were offered in exchange. We were nice about it, always said yes, and threw them in the trash the minute the girls turned their backs.

I visited the house where The Beatles were staying in Los Angeles. It was a classic, Hollywood luxury pad in Benedict Canyon, stocked with

the most beautiful, skimpily-clad groupies, the best dope, and the most suit-and-tie record company executives, trying very hard to look like they weren't trying at all. David Crosby, Steve Stills, Graham Nash, Mama Cass, Joan Baez and God knows who else was there. The atmosphere was thick with Significance. I left.

The plane rides were the only time I had to relax. All the bands and support personnel travelled together, along with all the equipment. That would never be the case these days, but everything was on such a smaller scale back them, it was feasible. One image that is still vivid in my mind is Neil Aspinall, The Beatles' road manager, sitting in the back, signing Beatles autographs on 8 x 10 glossies. He could forge all four signatures incredibly well.

The charter plane back from San Francisco to L.A., at the end of the tour, was an ancient wreck. Apparently, this was its last flight — it was on its way to an airplane junkyard. Some people didn't trust it at all, and elected to drive, or take a commercial flight. We spent the whole flight with our hearts pounding — it sounded like it was going to go down any minute. Of course, we self-medicated liberally to ease the anxiety.

made that remark about The Beatles being more popular than Jesus, and he was getting a lot of flak for it. He was really afraid that somebody was going to kill him.

I remember going up to The

Beatles' suite in the hotel in Toronto. Brian Epstein, The Beatles' manager, came over to the States with a huge cigarette box full of pre-rolled joints. He smoked them in a cigarette holder, took a puff or two and tossed them

Don Dannemann
Guitarist, vocal
The Cyrkle

■ At the first concert I remember being really nervous about playing at a Beatles' concert and worrying about everybody only wanting The Beatles. Oh God, how could we possibly get up and play with everybody yelling. "We want The Beatles! We want the Beatles!" The first concert was in Chicago at an indoor arena. I remember they announced The Cyrkle; we went on, and everybody whooped and hollered. We did our stuff and everybody seemed to like us. They didn't seem to be yelling, "We want The Beatles! We want The Beatles!" We did okay and felt good about that.

When we finished, I remember standing backstage. Backstage was essentially in the bleachers immediately behind the stage. I was standing by the railing overlooking the stage, anxiously awaiting The Beatles since we hadn't seen them or met

them yet. We were as much nervous fans as anyone else.

I remember, when The Beatles came out, it was one of the most magical moments I've ever had in my life. I hadn't (yet) seen them. They were our idols, and here they were. They were wearing these dark green velvet jackets; I remember they looked very cool.

We watched The Beatles from backstage, looking out over the audience. The first couple of rows we could see pretty clearly. I remember watching some girls, and it was as if they had electric shock machines underneath their chairs. You could look at any girl, and every ten seconds or so, it was as if somebody hit the button; the electricity went off, and she'd leap out of her seat! I mean it was like "vweeep," "vweeep." It was like a constant barrage of "vweeep," "vweeep" just watching them, you could see it pretty clearly.

Because it was an indoor arena, all that energy was trapped inside. I was standing next to an older woman. I was twenty-two or twenty-three at the time, and this woman was somewhere in her thirties or forties or whatever, and that was like an older woman to me at that time. I don't know who she was, but I remember glancing over to her at one point during the concert, and tears were just streaming down her face. It was just

that the energy was so intense that you got caught up in it!

After the first concert, we had seen them, but we hadn't met them yet. Everybody was so excited, wondering when we were actually going to meet "the boys." We were on the plane from Chicago to the next place. As you remember, we were all in the same plane. But, they were in the back of the plane behind a door. They had put a little wall up there so that they had their own private room in the back of the plane. On the first flight, that's how it was.

I was sitting with Tommy Dawes and our co-manger, Nat Weiss. We were chatting and just having a good old time and, of course, we kept looking back, wondering if somebody was gonna come out of that door. And, during this whole flight, we're just talking and talking and looking back and looking back. Finally, somewhere late in this flight, there's Paul. He's the one guy that came out. And, he's very slowly working his way up the aisle of the plane, and he's saying hello to people and meeting people. You could see that some people he's meeting for the first time, and a lot of people I guess he knew. You could see it was casual chatting, that kind of thing. We were trying to be very nonchalant about it; you look, and there he is, and you talk a little bit, and then you look back, and he's up a little

closer now. Anyway, he finally gets up to us, and he knows Nat Weiss. And, as you know, Nat was a good friend of Brian Epstein. They had formed a management company, and were our managers. Paul said hello to Nat, and they shook hands. Then, Nat intoduces Tommy and me to Paul McCartney.

The rest of the flight we talked about every little word that was said at that meeting, and what we could have done to have been cooler to engage him in a conversation that would have kept him there longer!"

CREDITS

Photos are credited as they appear in individual chapters.

Illustrations of venues by Tom Funk

Beatle ticket photos courtesy of Jeff Augsburger. *Beatle Memorabilia Price Guide* was authored by Jeff Augsburger, Marty Eck and Rick Rann ($15.00 ppd.) For more information, contact Jeff at 507 Normal Ave., Normal, IL 61761 or phone (309)452-9376.

Additional tickets provided by "Bojo" Bob, whose catalog of Beatle memorabilia is available at P.O. Box 1203, Cranberry Township, PA 16033.

Thanks also to...
Cliff Yamasaki and Let It Be Records, 2434 Judah, San Francisco, CA 94122. p/f (415) 681-2113.

Mark Naboshek for his support and contributions. Mark is a long-time Beatle collector who can be reached at: 6601 Clearhaven Circle, Dallas, TX 75248.

Barry Hood, producer of "Live in San Francisco," a one hour documentary. For information call 1-800-2-VIDEOS.

Gary Sohmers of Wex-Rex Memorabilia, Hudson, MA. tel. (508) 620-6181.

CREDITS

Photos are credited as they appear in individual chapters.

INTRODUCTION
Ed Freeman; Jamie Adams; Jamie Adams; Don Dannemann; Marty Fried and Earle Pickens; Marty Fried and Earle Pickens; *Go* Magazine.

CHICAGO
Peter J. Schulz/City Of Chicago; Photo by Jamie Adams; Astor Towers Condominium Association; *Teen Scene* Magazine; Associated Press/World Wide Photos; Ed Freeman. Article: "A Sound Analysis," *Chicago Sun Times*, August 13, 1966. Glenna Syse. Reprinted with permission. Chicago Sun Times, Copyright 1995.

DETROIT
Courtesy of General Motors Corporation, Copyright 1978, GM Corp. Used with permission; American Airlines Photo; Bob Wimmer; Ed Freeman; Bob Wimmer; Bob Wimmer; Bob Wimmer; Bob Wimmer; Bob Wimmer. Article: "30,800 Jam Beatlefest At Olympia," *Detroit News*, August 14, 1966. Jackie Korona. Reprinted with permission.

CLEVELAND
Mark C. Schwartz/Convention and Visitors Bureau of Greater Cleveland; UPI/Bettman; Renaissance Cleveland Hotel; Barry Tashian; Marty Fried and Earle Pickens. Article: "3,000 Fans Rush Stage, Force Beatles to Retreat," *Cleveland Plain Dealer*, August 15, 1966. Kenneth J. Moynihan. Reprinted with Permission.

WASHINGTON, D.C.
Superstock; Archive Photos; Courtesy of the Shoreham Hotel; Marty Fried and Earle Pickens. Article: "Beatles Sneak in for Half-Hour Show With Barely A Screech From 32,164," *Washington Post*, August 16, 1966. Copyright 1966, The Washington Post. Reprinted with permission.

PHILADELPHIA
Mike Roberts/Berkeley; Marty Fried and Earle Pickens; Archive Photos; Marty Fried and Earle Pickens; Marty Fried and Earle Pickens. Article: "20,000 Greet Beatles," *Philadephia Inquirer*, August 17, 1966. Rose DeWolf. Reprinted with author's permission.

TORONTO
Courtesy of Metro Parks and Culture, Toronto, and Andrew Colebeck; Bruce Turner/Turnerphoto; King Edward Hotel and Lance Blair; Ed Freeman; Tony Spataro. Article: "St. John Crew Treats 167 Cases As Young Fans Pursue Their Idols" *Toronto Globe And Mail*; August 19, 1966. Reprinted with permission from The Globe And Mail.

CREDITS

Photos are credited as they appear in individual chapters.

BOSTON

Greater Boston Convention and Visitor's Bureau; Used by permission of the Boston Public Library; Ed Freeman; Pete Anastasi, Jr./Boston, Mass.; Archive Photos; Pete Anastasi, Jr./Boston, Mass.; Bruce Turner/Turnerphoto; Pete Anastasi, Jr./Boston, Mass. Article: "25,000 Teens Cheer Beatles At Suffolk," *The Boston Globe*, August 19, 1966. Sara Davidson. Reprinted courtesy of The Boston Globe.

MEMPHIS

Memphis/Shelby County Public Library and Information Center; UPI/Bettmann; Marty Fried and Earle Pickens; *Teen Set* Magazine. Article: "Bang Joins Shrieks in Beatle Show," *The Commercial Appeal*, August 20, 1966. Copyright, 1966. The Commercial Appeal, Memphis, TN. Reprinted with permission.

CINCINNATI

Photo by Vince Re/Courtesy of Cincinnati Convention and Visitor's Bureau; Reggie Mays; Vernon Manor; Fred Straub; Fred Straub; Fred Straub; Fred Straub; Fred Straub; Fred Straub; Fred Straub. Article: "Double-Header With The Beatles," *The Cincinnati Post And Times-Star*, August 22, 1966. Dale Stevens. Reprinted with permission.

ST. LOUIS

St. Louis Convention and Visitor's Commission; Mark Richman; Mark Richman; Mark Richman; Mark Richman; *The American Heritage Dictionary of The English Language*. Copyright 1992 by Houghton Mifflin Company.. Article: "The Beatles Sing In The Rain For Wet, Enthusiastic Audience," *St. Louis Post-Dispatch*, August 22, 1966. Robert K. Sanford. Reprinted with permission.

NEW YORK

Municipal Archives, City of New York; Mel Tashian; UPI/Bettmann; Archive Photos; Andy Babiuk; Archive Photos, *Go* Magazine; UPI/Bettmann. Article: "The Beatles Bring Shea To A Wild Pitch Of Hysteria," *The New York Times*, August 24, 1966. Paul L. Montgomery. Reprinted by permission.

SEATTLE

Photo by John Wiley, Courtesy of Space Needle Corporation; Courtesy of Hugh Jones, Cellophane Square Records; Courtesy of The Edgewater Hotel. Article: "Beatles Storm City For Top One-Day Gross," *Seattle Post-Intelligencer*, August 24, 1966. Rolf Stromberg. Reprinted courtesy of the Seattle Post Intelligencer.

CREDITS

Photos are credited as they appear in individual chapters.

LOS ANGELES

Los Angeles Convention And Visitor's Bureau/Copyright 1991, Michele and Tom Grimm; Marty Fried and Earle Pickens; Cliff Yamasaki/Let It Be Records, San Francisco; *Teen Life Magazine; Teen Life Magazine;* Marty Fried and Earle Pickens; Ed Freeman; Ed Freeman; Ed Freeman; Ed Freeman; Ed Freeman; Ed Freeman; Ed Freeman. Article: "Adult Takes In A Concert," *Los Angeles Times*, August 29, 1966. Jack Smith. Reprinted with permission.

SAN FRANCISCO

Gordon Blackley; Barry Hood; UPI/Bettmann; Marty Fried and Earle Pickens; Ed Freeman; Ed Freeman. Article: "Beatles Strike Out At Ball Park," *San Francisco Examiner*, August 30, 1966. Reprinted with permission, San Francisco Examiner. "The Beatle Tour" by Rochelle Reed. KRLA's *BEAT Magazine.*

CONCLUSION

Jim McGuire; Marty Fried and Earle Pickens; Ed Freeman; Don Dannemann; Beaphoto, Hudson, MA.

Author's photo by Karl Hoffer.

Barry Tashian is a musician and songwriter living in Nashville, Tennessee. He and his wife, Holly, have two sons, Daniel and Carl.